Praise for Practical Reiki ™

"Practical Reiki ™ is a 'must have' for any energy worker, novice to advanced. Master teacher Alice Langholt presents pure Reiki: powerful, clear, concise, as it was meant to be. The reader is transported to a front row seat in Alice's classroom to learn, to be inspired, and become transformed. Highly recommend."

Connie Dohan, author *You Are Energy, Energy Healing 101*

"Alice's passion for Reiki shines through each word in *Practical Reiki ™.* Her fun and energetic teaching style will appeal to all. Whether you're just becoming interested in energy healing or are an advanced healer, this book should be included in your library. This refreshing modality stands alone or can be combined with any other energy healing method. I use it regularly along with Quantum Touch in my own practice, and have been impressed with the results."

Ernie Betz, Creekside Healing

"As an advanced bodyworker I have found Practical Reiki ™ to be quite useful by itself or in conjunction with other bodywork and massage techniques. The system is simple and easy to use."

John Goad, E.M.P., A.M.P, Head 2 Toe Massage

Alice Langholt

Practical
Reiki ™

for balance, well-being, and vibrant health

by Alice Langholt
Reiki Master Teacher

A guide to a simple, revolutionary
energy healing method.

Edited by Jennafer Martin and Don Beckett
Cover art by Alice Langholt

DEDICATION

I dedicate this book to Evan, my soul mate.
Thank you for believing in me, even when the
things I did seemed strange.

CONTENTS

ABOUT THIS BOOK

Why would I want to read this book?
If you've never heard of Reiki, this book will explain it in plain, clear language.

Reading the book will help you understand what Reiki is, how it works, how it helps, and how you can learn it. This book presents a down-to-earth, grounded approach that's easy to understand whether you've had any experience with intuition or none at all. *Anyone who wants to learn to connect with the innate, natural power for healing is capable of doing so.*

I'm already a Reiki Practitioner/Master. What's in this book for me? If you already practice Reiki, this book will show you the true essence of working with energy, beneath the ritual, symbols, and mystery surrounding the practice. It will widen your knowledge and strengthen your connection.

What is Practical Reiki ™ ? Practical Reiki ™ is a new, revolutionary Reiki modality for everyone who wishes to quickly and easily learn to practice Reiki energy healing for themselves and others. It is simple, strong, and will change your life. The entire method through Master level can be learned in just three weeks.

Will I be able to practice Practical Reiki ™ after reading this book? This book is the manual for the Practical Reiki ™ method. In order to become a practitioner or teacher of Practical Reiki ™, one needs to receive attunements and training from a Practical Reiki ™ Master, a person empowered to pass on this ability. It can be learned in person or via distance. The Internet is a good resource for finding a Practical Reiki ™ Master who could teach you. Reading this book will not provide the necessary attunements to be a Practical Reiki ™ practitioner or Master teacher. For a list of qualified and recommended Practical Reiki ™ teachers, refer to the ReikiAwakening.com website.

What about "regular Reiki"/ Usui Reiki/ Karuna Reiki ™ and other methods? This book does not go into detail about the history of Reiki, the practice, symbols or rituals used in Usui Reiki or other Reiki methods. There are many other books devoted to those subjects, as well as information widely found online.

Will learning Reiki help me heal myself? Although Reiki can help improve your health in physical, emotional and spiritual ways, Reiki is intended as a complementary approach to general health care and well-being. It is not meant to replace medical care or treatments. Always consult with your doctor before making any changes to your prescribed medical care.

ACKNOWLEDGMENTS

These people were guides along my journey, each contributing significantly to making this method and book possible. I am forever grateful.

My first Reiki teacher, Tamar Geri, who introduced me to Reiki. I am forever changed and my life has illuminated meaning because she approached me that day at our children's school.

Ole Gabrielsen, founder of Kundalini Reiki, who gave me his blessing to develop Kundalini Reiki into Practical Reiki, and whose method taught me to understand Reiki in a deep and meaningful way.

My mentor, Connie Dohan, who encouraged me, gave me business advice, and knew that I would be teaching Reiki long before I did.

My wonderful students, with their infinite wisdom and light, who allowed me to share some of their stories, gave me feedback on these techniques and methods, and filled my life with a constant stream of inspiration, encouragement, gratitude, and blessings.

FOREWORD

I am not special. I learned Reiki when I was 38 years old, after having no previous intuitive abilities at all, and spending most of my life wishing that I did. Having the experience of physically feeling the energy changed my life. It gave me a tangible connection to spiritual energy— something I had been seeking since I was a child. When that happened, I couldn't get enough. Reiki became the "super power" I had always wished for, and I embraced it completely.

Three months after completing my Usui Master Teacher training, I went on to learn a modality called Kundalini Reiki, developed by Ole Gabrielsen. This Reiki method helped refine my understanding of how Reiki energy works, the function of structure and ritual, and much more. It is this method on which Practical Reiki is based. Kundalini Reiki uses simple intention (more on intention in chapter 2), without the use of formal hand positions or symbols. Working with this method showed me that intention is the basis of all energy work.

The more I worked with and taught Kundalini Reiki, the more I realized that this method is extremely strong, simple, and practical. I developed a comprehensive manual to give my students a clear understanding of how to use Kundalini Reiki. My manual also became the manual of choice for Ole Gabrielsen. We taught an introduction class together online, he in Denmark, and I in the United States.

I thought about Reiki all the time, as my own experience led me to understand that it's really about being attuned and then being shown lots of ways to direct this healing energy. I looked at all of the ways I had been using Reiki in my own life, and how beneficial it is to me.

I have four children. I noticed the many ways Reiki was helping me care for them and myself. I wanted to show other parents how helpful Reiki could be for them too, so I created a curriculum called Reiki for Parents. I also created Reiki for Teens, Reiki for Kids, Reiki for Nurses and Caregivers, and Reiki for Pet Lovers. There are so many ways to utilize Reiki in one's life, and I wanted to make the uses clear to as many people as possible.

As I started offering Reiki healing in wellness centers and The Cleveland Clinic, I was told that the word "Kundalini" has some connotations that make some people uncomfortable. I also realized that the method could be taught without emphasizing the word Kundalini at all, besides in notes. So here, for your reference, are the basics on Kundalini.

Kundalini refers to energy that comes up from the earth, joining the Reiki energy which enters via the crown chakra. It can be easily referred to as "Earth energy," which is how it will be referred to in this text. The earth has a frequency of energy that relates to all living things. It is healing and grounding (restoring our connection to the earth when we place our intention there). This combination of Reiki and Earth energy creates a strong energetic frequency that is an extremely effective healing method, while being simple to learn and practical to practice.

Here's more on Kundalini: Kundalini energy also exists in all living beings when we are born. It is located encased in a ball-like energetic pocket at the base of the spine. As we go through life, some of us begin to seek intuitive growth and/or spiritual connection. This varies greatly by the age and intensity in which we work on our spiritual selves. As we start to gain access to our intuitive abilities, this Kundalini energy, which has been lying dormant since our birth, begins to gently release, subtly winding its way around the spine and chakras to the crown, connecting the Earth energy with the Divine energy that comes in from above. The process is not usually consciously felt, but for some, it is noticeable. It is the process of Enlightenment. This is called Kundalini Awakening.

You may have heard of an "improper" or "premature" Kundalini Awakening. A **very rare** condition has happened to a very small number of people whose Kundalini energy has risen too quickly, causing a feeling of disconnection from their physical bodies. This disconnect can create a mental imbalance. The imbalance can be disturbing enough to disrupt an individual's ability to work or care for himself or his family.

An improper Kundalini Awakening of this type can be caused by **intense continuous** intuitive practices such as a prolonged intensive meditation retreat, Kundalini Yoga practice of a prolonged and intense nature, psychotropic drug abuse, or an intense emotional trauma.

Two things are important to know about this Reiki method, formerly called Kundalini Reiki: 1) Practical (Kundalini) Reiki **does not cause an improper Kundalini Awakening**, and 2) Practical Reiki **will help heal someone who has suffered from an improper Kundalini Awakening**. The combination of Reiki and Earth energy in this method helps gently realign a person's energy with his physical body, grounds and heals the imbalance. I have personally attuned several people who suffered from an improper Kundalini Awakening to Practical (Kundalini) Reiki, and they all experienced relief and healing from their symptoms, going on to lead a normal life afterward.

Whether you call it "Kundalini" energy or "Earth energy," and whether you call it Practical Reiki, or Kundalini Reiki, beyond the terminology, what's most important here is knowing that: 1) energy is directed by intention, and 2) intention can be expressed in many ways. These important points will be emphasized and clarified in this book.

In order to make Reiki clear and accessible to everyone, this book is a guide to how Reiki practice can be simple, integrated into everyday life, and taught to others. It is a textbook on Reiki itself, and also a manual for the method known as Practical Reiki. Whether you use it as an informational resource or a textbook, it is my hope you find it useful. Many of the techniques of Practical Reiki can be used in conjunction with any other Reiki method. Becoming attuned to Practical Reiki will also strengthen any Reiki system you're already using.

1

THE BASICS

The method of energy healing known as Reiki was discovered by Mikao Usui in Japan in 1922. Usui received the knowledge of how to direct energy for healing during a 21 day fast and meditation on a mountain. Since Mikao Usui was the founder of the original version of Reiki, his method became known as Usui Reiki.

The word Reiki is a combination of two Japanese Kanji, the symbols used in Japanese to express meaning. Kanji are not words, but they serve the same function. The first, "Rei," means "guided." The second, "Ki," is the symbol for "life force energy." Some call it "universal energy." Whatever you call it, this is the energy that is our consciousness, our awareness of being alive. It comprises our thoughts, emotions, memories, and the way in which we experience everything about living.

The difference between your body and your life force energy is easily understood this way: consider a person who is alive, and then dies. The same physical material—his body, is still there. His life force energy departs, or separates, from his body at the time of transition (death).

This life force energy is integrated into our physical aspect as well. An example of this is that stress, an emotion, can make a person physically unwell. It is commonly understood that many digestive issues, ulcers, migraine headaches, and muscle tension can result from high stress levels. Similarly, our physical condition can affect our emotional state. For example, one who is in chronic pain may become depressed from the struggle of dealing with this pain day after day.

A person's life force energy can become imbalanced in many ways. One way is emotionally. Stress, depression, anger, fear, worry, jealousy, and frustration are just some of the ways that emotional energy can be blocked or deficient. Being in emotional balance means that we simply feel better, more capable, and handle the stress of life more easily.

Another way that life force energy can become imbalanced is physically. Pain is an example of a physical imbalance. Another is illness, which represents a manifestation of an energetic imbalance on a physical level. All illness begins in the energetic field.

You may wonder, "What about catching a cold? Isn't that just a germ?" If your immune system is weakened by an energetic imbalance, it won't be able to adequately fight off the germ that causes a cold, and you may catch it. The immune system needs a certain amount of personal energy to fuel it. It can run at peak efficiency if one's personal energy isn't being diverted to fighting stress, fatigue, or pain. Therefore, it is desirable to be as balanced as possible for optimum well being. Since I started practicing Reiki self healing daily, my health has improved, and I have found that I become ill very infrequently. When I do get sick, Reiki helps me feel better and recover faster than I used to before I learned Reiki. Simply put, the immune system functions better when a person is in balance.

Now the "Rei" part of Reiki – "guided" – how is that done? Energy is "guided" by **intention**. Intention is the "driver" for the energy. Intention is the way in which we tell the life force energy how we would like it to work. There are many ways that Reiki can work for us, including self healing, healing for others, healing relationships, clearing a room, sending energy to open opportunities for prosperity, and much more. We all have the ability and the power to direct intention the way we want to. Realizing this is a very important shift in thinking for most people who feel that life "just happens" to them.

A good analogy is to think of a driveway with some potholes here and there. Envision taking a bucket of water and sloshing the water over the driveway. The water will naturally collect in each hole as it runs over the driveway. When a hole fills, the extra water will move on to the next hole or run off. Each hole receives what it needs to fill up to the level of the driveway, and no more. You do not need to go to each individual pothole and pour water into it.

Compare this driveway analogy with your personal energy. In places you have stress or pain, emotional blockages, etc. These are your "potholes," or imbalances. Reiki energy is the water in this analogy. It will naturally fill in where you need it to as you intend for the energy to flow.

One important note is that you will only receive energy where you are ready to do so. Some people are consciously or unconsciously holding on to their imbalances, because these issues are protecting or serving them somehow. For instance, a man who had a recent divorce may be very angry and hurt. He is holding on to his anger to avoid dealing with the pain of the breakup. So if his anger were to be healed and released, he would need to deal with the pain beneath it all. He may not be ready to do that. So no matter how much one might think he needs Reiki to restore his emotional balance, he may not be ready to feel the depth of his pain. It's just easier for him to be angry right now. If I were to give this man Reiki, he might feel less angry for a while, but the anger would soon return shortly after our session until he decides that he is tired of being angry all the time, and he wants to feel better.

Another example is of "Mrs. Smith", who has chronic pain in her knees. Her son, "Joe", comes over and cares for her. He brings over groceries, sits and talks with his mom, and takes care of little fix-it needs in the house. Mrs. Smith loves his company and is grateful for her son's help. She subconsciously worries that if she were feeling better, Joe would not come around nearly as often, since she would be able to do more for herself. So getting better, having relief from the chronic knee pain that limits her, equates with less time with Joe. Mrs. Smith is receiving a gain from her pain. If Joe sets her up with a Reiki session, she will likely block the energy, and report that it didn't work for her. So even though Mrs. Smith needs Reiki for balance, to relieve her pain and help encourage her knee to heal, she is not emotionally ready for that to actually happen. We're complex creatures!

You may be wondering how a person becomes capable of being a Reiki practitioner to begin with. Everyone starts out as someone capable of receiving Reiki. In order to give Reiki to yourself or another person, you need an **attunement.** An attunement is a shift in your energy field, facilitated by one at the Master level of Reiki training, that opens the ability for you to direct the Reiki energy yourself.

Can you attune yourself to Reiki? Yes, but you would be choosing a more difficult path. Think of yourself as a radio. You want to play the Reiki channel. You don't know what it sounds like or where it's located on the dial. You could scroll through each frequency, straining to get it in clearly, and try to figure out if it's the channel you want. It would be difficult, but you might be able to find it eventually, and over time, tune in clearly to the Reiki channel yourself. Or, in an instant, a Reiki Master could set you to the exact frequency you need to get an immediate, unmistakably clear connection. It's literally that easy.

An attunement to Practical Reiki is given and received by intention. The intention of the Reiki Master to give the attunement, combined with your intention to receive the attunement. Neither of you need to concentrate, meditate, perform elaborate rituals, burn incense, play music, chant, say magic words, or do anything besides intend for the attunement to happen. Some Reiki methods require many steps, symbols, holding one's breath, blowing on the person being attuned, and even holding in the pelvic floor muscle the entire time as part of the process of giving an attunement. While those rituals may make the process a more formal, complex, and some may say "sacred" one, none of those would do a thing without intention. All that's really and truly needed to give and receive an attunement is the combined intention of the Reiki Master and the recipient. Whether you choose to add one, two, ten, or fifteen ritualized steps into the process really won't change, strengthen, or have any effect at all on the attunement itself. The attunement itself, created by intention, is what empowers a person to practice Reiki.

After receiving the level 1 attunement, one could be called a Practical Reiki Practitioner at level 1. After receiving the level 2 attunement, one is a Practical Reiki Practitioner at level 2. The level 3 attunement is the Master level attunement which empowers one to give attunements and use the title Practical Reiki ™ Master.

Now a word about the designation "Reiki Master." A Reiki Master is neither a guru nor necessarily an expert in Reiki. "Master" is the level of attunement and practice given to one who is now capable of passing on attunements to others. Reiki Master Teacher is a person at the master level of attunement who chooses to teach and attune others. It is best to select a Reiki Master Teacher who also chooses to practice Reiki in a mindful way—with regular self healing, and a regular Reiki practice. After all, you wouldn't go to a doctor who didn't take care of himself or regularly practice medicine, would you? A Reiki Master isn't a master of Reiki any more than a person with a Master's degree is a guaranteed genius. We're all human and make choices how to live our lives. Obviously, one hopes that a person who has chosen to become a Reiki Master will be dedicated to mindful and ethical Reiki practice. But, it's a good idea to choose a Reiki teacher who you recognize as a role model and mentor.

The best Reiki teachers will consider themselves your teacher/mentor for life if you wish it. They are invested in your success and confidence using Reiki, because they themselves feel a love, confidence and success with Reiki and want to offer the same to you. They are not simply interested in passing along attunements and sending you on your way. Instead, they consider themselves your guide into discovering your own intuitive journey and access to the healing power inside you. They want to help you awaken and train you. They want to be sure you are capable of doing the same for others, should you decide to be a Reiki teacher yourself someday. Choose a Reiki teacher based on these qualities, rather than who charges the least or who is the nearest to your location.

Regarding choosing to learn Reiki by distance or locally: two equally important factors should be considered. First, how do you prefer to learn? Reiki can be taught effectively either way, and attunements, like Reiki healings, are equally effective when given by distance as locally. If you like to be in the same room with your teacher, having in-person instruction, then seek a teacher in your local area. If you prefer to learn independently, or find that more practical for your own schedule or no teachers are available in your vicinity, then you can feel confident selecting a teacher who offers training via distance. Second, who is the teacher? Refer again to the previous paragraph on the qualities of an effective teacher. Whether teaching by distance or in person, the right teacher will be invested in your confidence and success in learning and practicing Reiki.

Obviously, money is a consideration for many people. And Reiki teachers will set their own fees. So you may be wondering if one who offers free attunements is as good or better than one who charges several hundred dollars. How much to charge is a very individual decision, based on many factors which may not be immediately apparent to the person shopping for a Reiki teacher. Teaching Reiki is a profession, as much as teaching Middle School is, and quality Reiki teachers think of themselves as professionals in their field. They deserve to be treated as such. That isn't to say that the most expensive Reiki training is the best. Only that if you wish, when you become a Reiki teacher someday, to offer attunements for free, then do so. If you wish to receive Reiki training for free, you will be able to find teachers that will teach without charge. The point is: reserve judgment of quality to quality itself, and don't tie it to fee structure. When selecting a teacher, choose the teacher first, and the money as less of a priority. If you have found the teacher you want and the fee is too high for your means, you can always ask the teacher if bartering or a payment plan is an option. Many Reiki teachers are open to making arrangements in order to make learning Reiki possible for all who wish to learn from them.

There are five ideals associated with Usui Reiki. They are called the Reiki Precepts, or Reiki Principles. While Reiki is not a religion, these ideals were developed by Mikao Usui to help his students meditate on the mindset of living an ethical and happier life. I think they are beautiful, simple and complex at the same time. Each can be meditated on individually, or the list of five can be strived for in daily life. I include them here because while they are not an essential part of actual Reiki practice, they can truly improve your life if you incorporate them into your thoughts.

The Reiki Precepts

The secret method of inviting blessings
The spiritual medicine of many illnesses
For today only, do not anger, do not worry.
Be grateful. Honestly do your work. Be kind to all people.
In the morning and at night, with hands held in prayer,
think this in your mind, chant this with your mouth.
The Usui Reiki method to change your mind and body
for the better.

The founder, Mikao Usui

The briefest form is this:

Just for today:
Avoid anger
Avoid worry
Work honestly
Be grateful
Be kind.

Simple. Complex. Profound. Just think what a better world this would be if people strived to accomplish these five ideas daily.

2

INTENTION AND ATTENTION, OR DON'T PUSH THE CAB

I mentioned in chapter 1 that intention is the means for directing Reiki energy, so let's talk about what intention is, to be clear. Intention can be defined as **directed thought**. Intention is what you mean to happen. It's more than a hope or a desire, although it could be defined as thinking toward a desired outcome. Intention can be expressed in many ways, the simplest among them being directed thought. It's "thinking loudly" or "thinking specifically" rather than daydreaming. Another simple way to express intention is through speaking. Giving directions aloud is a way of expressing intention via speaking.

That may sound simple, and it is. Our thoughts and emotions are all made of energy. This energy can affect other people. You've probably had the experience of sensing another person's anger or sadness without that person having told you. Or "catching" another person's happy, bubbly mood after being around that person for a short while. Your energy isn't simply contained in that bubble of an aura of yours. It is also connected to all energy around and in every living thing. All living things and the Earth have life force energy. The Earth has a different vibrational energy, but it has energy too. Hard to believe?

Here's an analogy that could help. Think of life force energy like water. Water is a substance that exists everywhere around us: in the air we breathe, in our bodies, in the sky, seas, as dew on the grass, rain, fog, in fruit and vegetables, and we drink it. It also recycles itself into different forms, and through our bodies, animals, plants, and the ecosystem. The same amount of water exists on the planet now as far back as life existed on the Earth. Let yourself imagine all water molecules connected to each other, regardless of the form of water they embody. Fog, mist, liquid, ice, humidity, clouds, and water content of plants, blood, fluids, and gasses, are all connected to each other. All of these connected water molecules surround and penetrate the Earth and all life as one single interwoven being. Water is the perfect analogy for life force energy.

Life force energy is like water in this analogy. We may not think of it being between us where we don't see it (as humidity in the air), but it is there. Life force energy is also one connected entity. It exists in our bodies as water does—integrated into our cells, organs, breath, and digestive system, and also between, above, below, and around us. When our personal energy becomes off balance, when we have areas in which we are deficient or overactive, life force energy is available to help correct these places and bring us gently into balance. Reiki can restore balance. A

Reiki practitioner connects with this unlimited source of life force energy around us all, and intends for it to flow to the areas in need of balancing. That area or areas can be within oneself, or for another person, animal, plant, etc. It also can be sent over any distance or ahead in time, because neither space nor time are limitations when it comes to life force energy.

The way to guide the energy where we would like it to go is via intention. But it is important to know that intention is only needed for giving the energy a start in the right direction. After that, it's best to "get out of the way" and let the energy flow where the recipient is ready to receive it. This is similar to giving directions to a cab driver, and then letting that cab driver go to the intended destination. You don't need to push the cab along after giving directions. You can simply observe where the cab is going once you do. That part is called "attention."

When it comes to energy, all you need to do is to set the **intention**, and then place a gentle **attention** on where the energy is being received. An important point is that the practitioner is not as much a "healer" as a "facilitator of healing." The practitioner is offering the Reiki for the recipient to absorb wherever there is a need for balance. The energy does not "zap" out of the practitioner's hands. Reiki flows to the recipient by intention. The practitioner's hands and intuition only serve to inform the practitioner where the Reiki is going as the session is happening. There are no mandatory hand positions, but rather the hands become useful for focusing one's attention on the flow of the Reiki energy. Wherever the practitioner places his hands, he becomes aware of the ebb and flow of the Reiki in that area.

The recipient is the actual "healer," because he or she is the one doing the healing. For the practitioner, there's a beautiful dialogue between starting the Reiki flowing and noticing it is being received.

Here's an interesting example. One of my students sent a distance healing to a woman who had been suffering from neurological damage after a stroke. He intended for the Reiki energy to send healing to her brain. He hypothesized that the Reiki would help improve her test scores on an IQ test. My student wanted to test the effects of the Reiki by having the woman complete an assessment of intelligence on the computer before and after the Reiki session. He sent the Reiki, and her tongue, which had been off-center to the left since the stroke, suddenly moved back to the midline of her mouth, dramatically improving her diction. The Reiki healed the part of her brain that had been controlling the placement of her tongue. Did the Reiki follow my student's intention? Yes, it sent healing to the woman's brain. Did it produce his expected result? No, but it affected healing in the way in which she was ready to receive healing.

Here's another example: Jackie goes to receive a Reiki healing from Mari. Jackie lies down on the massage table. Mari intends to connect with the Reiki energy (see chapter

5 for more information on how to begin a Reiki healing) and asks in her mind for Jackie to receive the healing that is needed. Then, Mari simply places a gentle attention on what she feels as she moves her hands above Jackie's body. Mari notices different sensations as she does, including a stronger sensation over Jackie's heart area. "Have you been putting yourself last again, Jackie?" Mari asks gently. Jackie, a working mom who is a caregiver for her ailing father, simply laughs. Mari has sensed the imbalance between giving and receiving indicated by Jackie's receiving a strong flow of energy in her heart chakra (one of seven major energy processing centers – covered in chapter 4). Because Mari was simply placing attention on the nuances of the energy flow, she was able to notice Jackie's area of imbalance. More important, she and Jackie had a moment which brought Jackie's attention to her need for energy. Doing so enhanced Jackie's ability to receive the Reiki, as one will receive the healing for which one is ready. Mari wasn't "putting" the energy in Jackie's heart chakra when she noticed it flowing there. Mari was simply noticing that the energy was being received in that area. This is an important point which will be emphasized again in the next two chapters.

There are many ways to sense the Reiki energy flowing. Mindfully and regularly practicing Reiki will strengthen your intuition. The next chapter will explain how people become aware of intuitive information, including the flow of Reiki.

3

CLARITY ON CLAIRS

How does Reiki energy feel? How does one know when it's being received or when one is giving Reiki? First, let me mention that you do not need to be naturally psychic or sensitive to energy to learn Reiki. Everyone has natural healing abilities; they're a part of being human. Anyone who wishes can learn to connect and direct these abilities to heal oneself or direct healing to others.

In general, to most people, Reiki feels relaxing. That's pretty much across the board what one receiving a Reiki healing would experience. That's not all, but that seems to be just one benefit of receiving a Reiki healing. Beyond that, the sensations are varied and the benefits are received according to the needs and readiness of the individual receiving the energy.

Reiki feels different to different people because of the nature of how people are sensitive to energy. There are four main ways that people are naturally sensitive to energy. For most of us, one way is the strongest, and the others are at various levels from medium to very low. These ways of sensing energy are called **clairs**. Clair is a prefix which means "clear". All clairs are ways in which our intuition speaks to us.

The first clair (in no particular order) is called **clairvoyance**—"clear sight". You've probably heard that word and thought it referred to psychics who can see your dead relatives or your guardian angel. In fact, it refers to any visual intuitive sensitivity to energy. So if you close your eyes during Reiki, and see colors swirling, lights flashing, images appearing on your mind screen, that is your visual clair in action.

The second clair is called **clairaudience**—"clear hearing". This refers to any intuitive information that is received via the ears. Some people hear a gentle ringing, buzzing, or feel a vibration in their ears. My daughter, Sari, says that she hears quiet music when she gives or receives Reiki. Others may feel as if a voice is whispering guidance into their ear or ears. (Of course if the voices are telling you to commit any act of violence, this is not clairaudience, but a reason to get yourself to the ER.) The audient clair activates as a sign that the energy is flowing, and there may become different pitches, frequencies, or variations on the audient sounds. Each variation is a way in which the energy is giving you information. More about that will follow.

The third clair is called **clairsentience**—"clear feeling". This is intuitive information received via the sense of touch. Clairsentient sensations could be tingles, changes in temperature, a "magnetic" or "static"-like sensation, light feather touches on your face or hands, waves of energy, or any other feeling you would describe in a physical way. When I first started sensing Reiki energy, my hands started to tingle. I was amazed to find that when I held my hand over my teacher's hip, my hand tingled, and when I moved it, the tingling stopped. I did this several times, noting the consistency of the change. When I remarked about this, she told me that her hip was sore from a pulled muscle. The tingling I felt was a clairsentient response to her hip being energetically out of balance. Now my hands tingle every time I give Reiki, and there are many kinds of tingles that mean various things, such as pain, grief, blockages, and more. Think of Mari in the example in chapter 2. Mari's clairsentient response allowed her to enter into a dialogue with Jackie about Jackie's need for energy.

The fourth clair is called **claircognizance**—"clear knowing". This means knowing something without being sure just exactly where the information is coming from. For instance, if the phone rings, and you "just know" it's your mother calling. Or if you were thinking about a friend you haven't heard from in a long time, and you see that same person in a store the same day. Most of us have had claircognizant experiences from time to time. Sometimes we chalk them up to coincidence or say, "that was strange" afterward. If intuitive information is coming through your thoughts, that's your intuition communicating with you through claircognition.

Think of your intuition as a muscle, just like a physical muscle. The more you exercise it, the stronger it gets. There are many exercises for your intuition. Intuition-strengthening practices include meditation, yoga, Tai Chi, Qi Gong, and the many energy healing methods out there, including (of course) Reiki. For those who practice Reiki, mindful regular practice will naturally strengthen and fine tune their intuition, strengthening their clairs as part of the process.

Energy speaks to us in a subtle language through our primary or major clair, and also through our other clairs when we learn to access them. We learn to access them through mindful practice, as mentioned before. Also, when one clair gets stronger, the others usually do too, because they are all part of our intuitive abilities.

This subtle language can come as a range of sensations. For instance, for a clairvoyant person, red may appear, changing to green during a healing session. Images may appear in the practitioner's (or recipient)'s mind as well. The person giving the healing will learn to interpret the meaning of these sensations through experience.

If a clairsentient person is giving Reiki, she may at first experience tingles or heat in her hands. As time goes on, and she continues to practice Reiki regularly, there may be more sensations such as stronger tingles, faster or slower tingles, or other feelings. The practitioner will begin to notice consistencies in the sensations, such as a particular "zippy" tingle happens whenever the recipient has pain in the area in which the practitioner feels those zippy sensations. After much practice, the practitioner will notice that same "zippy" tingle and will ask her client if he has a pain where she feels that tingle. This is what happened for me as I practiced Reiki regularly.

Think of the subtle language of energy as you being air dropped into a foreign country and needing to learn to speak the language without a translation dictionary. You have to use your powers of observation (**attention**) to catch patterns in the foreign language. Soon you will start to connect these patterns with meaning. The longer you are there, the more times you hear certain words, the more they become familiar and meaningful to you. (By the way, this is also the way babies learn language.)

This analogy to foreign language relates to energy work directly. The energy speaks to you through your intuition, and your clairs are the way you experience this language. As you continue to work with Reiki, you'll feel more subtle sensations and start to identify patterns in them. Those patterns are the language of the energy. You are learning the vocabulary as you work with it.

It's important to note that even if you and I are both clairsentient, my "zippy tingle" may mean something different from your "zippy tingle." We each need to learn the language of our own intuition. There is not one guide to tell you what each kind of sensation means. Don't feel frustrated by this, though. It's a wonderful process of self-discovery that everyone should have the opportunity to experience. You really learn to tune in to your intuitive processes—become the observer—as you practice, and in doing so, you realize, strengthen and nurture your own intuition. You learn to trust your intuitive abilities too, which can lead to wonderful changes in your own life.

4

DEMYSTIFYING THE CHAKRAS

It is not necessary for you to know any of the information in this chapter in order to give or receive a Reiki healing. The simplest way to work with Reiki is to know that 1) You start the energy flowing by intention, and 2) the energy will be received where the recipient is ready to receive it. You can give an entire Reiki healing by simply placing your hands on or above the recipient's shoulders if you want, and the energy will flow to the places it is needed most (think of the driveway analogy in chapter 2). So you could skip this chapter if you want, and still learn enough from this book to give an effective Reiki healing after being attuned. But before you start flipping ahead, here's why this chapter may be useful to you.

As you start to become aware of your clairs and the intuitive information you are receiving, you can begin to sense the areas in a person that need and are taking in energy. It's good for your intuition—and useful for the recipient—for you to be able to notice these areas. You may wish to bring them to the attention of the recipient. You may simply wish to notice the change that you feel or sense when a particular area has received as much energy as needed. Noticing particular areas which are receiving or in need of energy is called "scanning." Scanning can be done in person or even via distance. Distance healing techniques will be covered in chapter 5.

As mentioned earlier, chakras are energy processing centers located in specific parts of the body, extending outward into the aura. There are seven main chakras, although there are many minor chakras and even some located above and below the physical body. This book will introduce the seven main chakras.

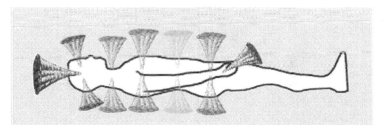

The chakras are shaped like funnels filled with smaller funnels inside them. Each smaller, inner funnel spins, and the main funnel of each chakra spins also. Chakras have a front and a rear. Picture the small part of the funnel going into the body, with the bigger outer part facing away from the body. This means that there are two funnels – a front and a rear – extending from the front and back of the body at the location of each chakra. Two exceptions are: the top (crown) and bottom (base) chakras do not have a front and back, but simply extend outward vertically from those points. (See illustration above.) The chakras spin in counter-clockwise motion in the front of the body, and clockwise in the rear of the body.

Most people can't see chakras, although the location and state of each chakra's health can be sensed via the intuitive clairs (covered in the previous chapter). When chakras are blocked or overactive, they require balancing. Providing Reiki can help bring them into balance. Since chakras are our energy processing centers, they are very important in helping maintain our overall health.

Each chakra processes a specific set of emotions. That set of emotions is different for each chakra. Each chakra also affects the physical body parts and organs in its relative area of the body. Each chakra responds to a specific color and musical note. This is why some people use crystals of different colors, tuning forks or singing bowls in their healing sessions.

Here is a primer on each chakra, its location and function. These basics are enough for you to get an understanding of what it could mean when you sense Reiki is being received in any of these areas. You can certainly go on to learn more about chakras from a book (such as *The Chakra Bible* by Patricia Mercier), a course, or any number of websites dedicated to information on chakras.

For the purposes of easy reference, there are two-word phrases that are useful in remembering the function of each chakra. The heading of each section below will include the number, name, phrase, and color for each chakra. You'll notice that the colors for the chakras match the order of the rainbow.

Chakra #1
Other name: The Base/Root Chakra
Phrase: "I Need"
Color: Red

This chakra, located at the lower pelvis, relates to the basic, primal will to live and those things needed for the basics of living (for example, food, water, clothing and shelter). When functioning normally, a person feels good about life and has what he needs to live. He also has a healthy way to maintain his sex drive. This chakra can be blocked or thrown off balance by severe depression, homelessness, starvation, eating disorders, or sexual abuse. It relates to the sexual organs (men), hips, legs and lower back. This chakra does not have a front and back, but rather extends downward and tilts forward at a slight angle from the groin.

Chakra #2
Other name: The Sacral Chakra
Phrase: "I Want"
Color: Orange

This chakra, located near the navel, relates to intimacy, abundance, and creativity. It's about being recognized as the unique, creative beings that we are. This recognition can come in the form of money, appreciation, and freedom of expression. Since it relates to creation, this also relates to procreation, and therefore the reproductive organs are involved. With intimacy, this could be with a sexual partner, or with those closest to us, such as our best friends, siblings, and parents. When we are being paid well for what we bring to our jobs, are recognized and appreciated for our unique skills, talents, and personalities, and have thriving close friendships and relationships, this chakra is in balance. It can become blocked or out of balance from job loss, relationship problems or breakups, or failing to give ourselves the opportunity for creative expression. This chakra's health can be represented physically in the menstrual cycle, male reproductive system, the upper hips, and the lower digestive system.

Chakra #3
Other name: The Solar Plexus Chakra
Phrase: "I Can"
Color: Yellow

This chakra is located at the solar plexus, at the center of the bottom of the rib cage. It relates to our personal sense of power and control over our lives. Feeling capable is important for our sense of security. It's easy to see how this chakra could be off balance due to stress or anxiety. Stress and anxiety happen when we feel that things are happening that we don't have control over, or we don't know what's going to happen next. When we feel that we can handle whatever comes, it's a lot easier to actually do so! The third chakra relates to the upper digestive system, including the stomach and upper intestinal tract, and the middle back. It's a well known fact that stress can cause ulcers and acid reflux, for example, muscle tension (in many places in the body), or simply an upset stomach. Reiki helps a person to relax, and relaxation releases stress.

Chakra #4
Other name: The Heart Chakra
Phrase: "I Love"
Color: Green

This chakra is located at the heart, in the center of the chest, rather than over the physical heart on the left side. It relates to giving and receiving love and care. This also relates to the self-esteem, in terms of feeling loveable yourself and allowing yourself to receive as well as give. Parents caring for kids, for their own parents, or those in caretaker jobs often have heart chakras in need of balancing. They simply give more than they receive, or they put themselves last, after caring for everyone else. Also, grief can cause this chakra to become blocked. Simple things can help keep this chakra in balance, such as remembering to eat well, breathe fully, exercise, and get adequate rest. Also, allowing others to help you, and remembering to take time for yourself each day can do wonders. Companionship is also important to heart chakra health, as loneliness indicates an imbalance in giving and receiving love and care. This chakra relates to the heart, respiratory system, and the upper back muscles as well. Note: you may have heard this chakra described as pink instead of green. That is because there is an "upper heart chakra" slightly above the heart chakra that is pink. Both heart chakras relate to love and care, and are subtly different in the scope of the relationships they deal with. For the purposes of this text, that's plenty.

Chakra #5
Other name: The Throat Chakra
Phrase: "I Express"
Color: Blue

This chakra is located at the throat, and it relates to communication. Communication goes both ways, giving and receiving. Those who hold back from saying what they are thinking because of fear of conflict, or other reasons, may have blocked throat chakras. If you feel you're having communication issues with a friend, parent, coworker, sibling, or spouse, there could be an imbalance in the throat chakra. Releasing blockages in the throat chakra can help you "find the words" to communicate more effectively. The throat chakra relates to the throat, thyroid, neck, jaw, and mouth.

Chakra #6
Other name: The Third Eye Chakra
Phrase: "I See"
Color: Indigo/ Purple

This chakra is located in the center of the forehead, and relates to the intuition. All clairs receive information through this chakra. All intuitive information is processed here. Feeling a sense of purpose in your life, feeling guided and supported, and feeling "intuitive" in general indicate a healthy sixth chakra. Conversely, if you feel like you have no idea what you should be doing with your life, that you have no purpose, or you feel "disconnected" from your intuition, this chakra may be blocked. Physically, this chakra relates to the eyes, ears, pineal gland, brain and head.

Chakra #7
Other name: The Crown Chakra
Phrase: "I Am"
Color: Purple/ White (or Clear)

This chakra is located at the top of the head, in the center. It does not have a front and back, but rather extends upward. It relates to a sense of "Divine connection," feeling connected to something outside yourself, to All That Is, and acknowledging that we are all spiritual beings having a human experience. The phrase "I Am" could be interpreted to mean "I am energy." It doesn't require one to be "religious," but it does relate to the spiritual self. If you feel disconnected from this spiritual aspect of yourself, you may benefit from some healing here. It is also important to note that Reiki energy enters through the crown chakra. It is the spiritual energy inlet for the energetic body when practicing Reiki.

Some notes about chakras:
- They go from the primal to the spiritual, in order from the bottom (base) to the top (crown).

- They have a front and a back. The front of the chakra reflects the current state of one's energy. The back reflects the past and cause of any imbalance.

- They can be healed by energy, color, sound, aromas, or a combination. Each method still sends a balancing intention to that particular chakra.

- They extend beyond the physical body into the aura.

- They can be sensed by the practitioner through his or her clairs, or can be located using a pendulum. (See Appendix B for how to use a pendulum.)

5

PRACTICAL REIKI LEVEL 1

Level 1 of Practical Reiki gives you the "meat and potatoes" of Reiki practice. This isn't "Reiki 101" or "low level Reiki." It is strong from the first level, unlike other Reiki methods which start out feeling relatively weak for some.

I will share that when I first learned Reiki, level 1 was so weak for me that for an entire year and a half I thought it wasn't working, and assumed that I wasn't any good at Reiki. I love Practical Reiki because none of my students have had that experience—they feel the energy from the very first second of their attunement, and can immediately feel and start using Reiki when their first attunement is finished. The ambiguity and doubt are eliminated. I never would have become a Reiki teacher if some of my students had felt as I did after my first attunement. I would never have felt confident enough to tell people that this would work for them. Thankfully, that wasn't the case, and as of this writing, I've taught over 450 people with 100% success.

Why do many people believe that Practical Reiki feels stronger than other Reiki methods? I suspect it has to do with the focus on intention without structure, allowing the practitioner to directly tune in to the energy. It may also have to do with the way Earth energy and Reiki energy combine in this method.

Whether my students were Reiki Master Teachers with years of experience, or completely new to Reiki, all felt the energy immediately. Practitioners of other Reiki or energy healing methods noted that the addition of Practical Reiki to their practice "super-charged" their energy and gave them freedom to direct the energy more quickly than before. It also gave them a more global understanding of Reiki and how it works.

The Level 1 Attunement

The level 1 attunement to Practical Reiki will enlarge your crown, heart, and palm chakras (minor chakras located in the palms of the hands), allowing the Reiki energy to flow freely through them. The Reiki energy enters through the crown chakra and flows through the body, directed by intention. (Information on chakras is found in chapter 4.) The Earth energy will be brought in to join the flow of Reiki during the level 2 attunement.

Regardless of whether your teacher is giving your attunement in person or by distance, the way you receive it is the same. To receive the attunements to Practical Reiki, you should relax comfortably in a quiet place. You may be seated, recline, or lie down. (If you fall asleep the attunement will still work, but it's more fun to be awake and experience the attunement consciously!) It's a good idea to rest your hands with palms facing up. This is a receptive posture and it helps you be in the mindset of openness. It is useful to close your eyes, because this allows you to tune in more fully, and also is easier for you to notice your visual clair. Then, simply intend to receive the attunement. You can do this by saying softly, "I am now receiving the Practical Reiki level (number) attunement" or simply think deliberately that you are ready for the attunement to begin. Then, just quietly observe how you feel. Your primary clair will likely bring the predominant sensations of the attunement. Whatever you feel, sense, hear or see, just observe with an attitude of wonder. Whether you feel a lot or nothing at all, if you intend to receive the attunement, you will. When you feel the attunement has ended, just open your eyes. You may feel it end abruptly, taper off, or you may simply feel a sense of closure. The attunements typically last for about 35 minutes. If you are in a classroom with other students, you may find that the students open their eyes around 12 minutes in. They usually are still feeling the attunement, but the presence of the other students around them makes them a little self-conscious. Alone, whether receiving the attunement in person or by distance, a student will usually take the full 35 minutes to enjoy the experience.

Attunements typically feel like a strong Reiki healing. While everyone is different in the specific ways they experience attunements, some of the sensations reported include: heat; pressure or tingles in the palms, chest, feet and/ or face; swirling colors which change; a feeling of swaying; quickening of the heartbeat; sensations moving through various parts of the body, hearing soothing messages, or feeling the presences of guides and angels. Afterward, most people feel really good, and are excited to start working with the Reiki energy.

Following attunements, one may feel a little "spaccy." This is called being "ungrounded" and it's a result of the higher chakras being activated by the attunement. Think of standing on your head and having the blood rush to your face. Energetically, you've just done that in a way. If you feel this way, it's a very good idea to do some grounding techniques to bring your energy back down to earth where it should be.

Here are some ways to ground your energy that are very useful:

- **Drink a big glass of water.** Water is very important for many reasons. An attunement is an energetic detox which can affect you emotionally, physically, and spiritually. Water has energetic and physical properties. Just as if you were doing a dietary cleanse, be sure to allow water to assist the detox process.

• **Get outdoors.** Take a walk outside. Stand, sit, or lie on the ground.

• **Do the Grounding Tree Meditation.** Stand firmly, feet shoulder width apart. Visualize, imagine, or pretend that you have roots growing down from the bottom of your feet into the Earth. Send those roots growing down deeper and deeper, all the way through the core of the Earth. They thicken and spread out fully. Then, visualize pulling Earth energy up those roots all the way back into your feet and up your body. Feel the energy move up your legs, torso, shoulders, down to your hands and back up your arms and shoulders, up your neck, face, and out the top of your head. Continue sending the energy upward as far as you can. Then pull it back down into the top of your head, face, neck, chest and into your heart, connecting the Reiki energy with the Earth energy. Breathe. This brief meditation can be practiced until it can be done within about 20 seconds. It is extremely effective. It is also good any time of day to immediately relieve stress and clear your thoughts when the day seems crazy. If you are sensitive to other people's emotions or energy, grounding your energy can help define and protect your own energetic boundaries. It is an important technique.

- **Take a bath with Epsom salts.** The combination of water and Epsom salt is very grounding. Salt, a mineral, is known to have grounding and protective qualities. Adding a Tablespoon of salt to a bath can offer this benefit.

- **Eat root vegetables such as carrots, potatoes, turnips, parsnips, etc.** Because they grow within the Earth, they are grounding. So is protein.

- **Do self healing often.** Activating Reiki can help your energy adjust.

About clearing symptoms

Rarely, some brief physical symptoms may occur after an attunement. They are part of the detoxification process and won't last more than a day or two if they do occur. They are known as "clearing symptoms." In my experience, only one percent of those I've attuned have experienced any clearing symptoms after an attunement, and those who did only had symptoms after the first attunement, not the second or third. It seems that the first attunement clears away some energetic sludge and may surprise the system a little with the readjustment. Clearing symptoms can include mild nausea, loose stools, emotional mood swings, or an over-energized feeling. They aren't really different from if you were doing a physical detoxification. Should you experience clearing symptoms, 1) don't be alarmed, 2) ground your energy often, and 3) give yourself Reiki often. Nurture yourself and get extra rest if you need it. Following the grounding procedures above will help the clearing symptoms resolve within 24-48 hours. Remember that you are beginning a powerful healing process and treat yourself with loving kindness.

Working with Practical Reiki level 1

As I mentioned earlier, level 1 gives the "meat and potatoes" of the Practical Reiki method. This "meat and potatoes" of Practical Reiki level 1 establishes the true foundation of Reiki practice. These are the healings you will use most often throughout your Reiki practice: self healing, healing for others, distance healing, clearing a room, karmic band (relationship) healing, and situation/ qualities healing.

- **Turn on the energy**

Any time you work with the Reiki energy, the first thing you do is to "turn it on." This is done by expressing (aloud or in thoughts) the intention to connect with the energy. Most people simply think "Reiki" or "Reiki on" to do this.

Note: it is an ethical practice to receive permission before giving or sending (distance) Reiki to another person. See chapter 9 for more on Reiki and Ethics.

- **The level 1 healings and how to activate them:**

Self healing

In Practical Reiki level 1, among the very first things you learn is self healing. This is the most important thing you can do with Reiki, and you should give yourself Reiki daily. Self healing improves your own health and gently exercises and strengthens your intuition also. Daily self healing with Reiki gives you the opportunity to use Reiki every day, regardless of whether you will do healings for another person. Daily practice will strengthen your ability to feel the energy and make you a more effective Reiki practitioner.

As mentioned above, begin by turning on the energy. Think "Reiki" or "Reiki on"!

The next thing you do is to intend what you want the Reiki to do. For self healing, this means you think (or say) "self healing." Then, put your hands on yourself anywhere you find comfortable. For a general self healing, this could be on your chest, stomach, or lap. Or just place them anywhere you want. If you have something that hurts, put your hands on the area that's hurting.

It's not that the energy comes shooting out of your hands. It doesn't. But your hands act as sensors, similar to a computer mouse, telling you (through your primary clair which compares to the computer monitor) that the energy is flowing. You may also receive various sensations that will give you information about how strong the energy is flowing, or if there are energetic blockages in a particular area. Putting your hands on yourself in a given spot will help you focus your attention on that place and you can receive information about the energy being received there as it's flowing.

Placing your hands on your head if you have a headache will also help you place your attention on your head, and tune you in to feeling the energy flowing there. Intentionally directing your attention there will increase your ability to be receptive to the energy, so you will receive it more effectively as a result.

With Practical Reiki, all you need to do once you turn on the energy and set your intention for self healing is to place your attention on the sensation of the energy as it flows. It will run on its own, and stop when it's done. Most practitioners feel the energy start and come to a close when finished. (Remember that the recipient will receive the healing in whatever way he or she is ready.) A Practical Reiki healing typically takes between five and seven minutes to give, but the energy will be received for about 35 minutes.

The effects of Reiki healing last longer than 35 minutes, of course. The effects of the healing session will be relative to the need for healing. In general, the longer you've had the problem, the longer it will take to improve it. Acute conditions or those which have just started will heal more quickly than chronic conditions that developed over a long period of time. Also, the more severe the issue, a number of healing sessions given frequently will be most effective at making a difference. But that's just a generality, and everyone is different. Never give up if you feel that results are happening slower than you'd like. The pace can vary, but there will be changes.

Another benefit of regular self healing with Reiki is that it gives you the opportunity to tune in to how you are feeling each day. So often we zoom through our day, barely aware of our own breathing, let alone how we feel emotionally and physically. Taking even five minutes to relax and give ourselves some Reiki can alert us to places in which we are tense or uncomfortable, and give us the chance to allow Reiki to gently bring us into balance again.

It can be beneficial to receive healing from another person as well as giving yourself regular self healing. Just relaxing into a healing given by another allows for a powerful healing session. But self healing is important enough to do every day. Think of self healing as keeping your car's engine maintained with oil changes and fluids, and receiving Reiki from another person as getting that professional tune up. Another analogy is massaging your own shoulder if it is sore, which can help, or going to a massage therapist for a treatment, which can be even more effective.

Hands-on Reiki for another person

To give a Reiki healing to someone else using Practical Reiki, the first thing you do is connect with the energy by intending "Reiki." (Remember, turn the Reiki on!) Then you can simply place your hands on or hover them over the person you are treating, and intend "the healing that is needed." There is no need to concentrate, meditate, or otherwise "try" to do anything. Just switch to "attention" mode and observe what you notice as the energy flows. Remember: don't push the cab.

The energy will flow for five to seven minutes, and then you will feel it stop or come to a close. You may have a sense of closure, or you may feel the energy simply "turn off" or "dwindle away." Regardless of which it is for you, it means your part is finished.

There are no "mandatory" hand positions in Practical Reiki. The energy will go wherever the person is ready to receive it. But your hands will serve as your sensors, giving you the chance to experience where the energy is flowing strongly depending on where you put them.

Some ideal places to put your hands include: over or on the recipient's shoulders, over or on the person's head, or hovering one hand in front and one hand in back of the center of the chest. Of course, if the person you're treating has pain somewhere, you can place your hands on or above the area where there's pain.

It's fine to either hover or place your hands on the person—it's simply your choice. The energy will flow either way. You may choose to do one or the other because you may feel the energy more strongly yourself when your hands are not touching the other person. Sometimes the tactile sense of touching a person's shirt, hair, or body will interfere with your subtle sensations of the energy flowing. It won't affect the recipient's ability to feel the energy either way. It may be useful to learn to feel the energy with your hands off first, and then you can try hands-on. If the person doesn't want to be touched, then of course don't touch. If the person would benefit from the reassurance of your touch, you may choose to do so. Or, you may choose to sometimes hover and sometimes touch, depending on where you place your hands. Any way or combination of ways is just fine. Let the situation and your intuition dictate which you choose.

You could offer the entire healing session with your hands above the recipient's shoulders, and trust that the energy will go wherever the person is ready for it. That's fine. But moving your hands around to some different places will give you the chance to experience the difference you feel at each place, so you'll be able to notice and comment (if appropriate) about what you feel. It's good exercise for your intuition if you tune in to the energy as you move your hands to different spots.

Pain, stress, grief, and illness will generally trigger a strong flow of Reiki, which you may notice. Your recipient may also feel powerful sensations at the same time that you do. A few minutes after you start, you may start to feel a decrease in the energy flow if you keep your hand on or above an area of concern. For example, if Joe has a sore knee, I might place my hands above his knee while the Reiki flows. At first, I might feel the energy strongly. After a few minutes, I may feel it change to a subtler sensation, indicating that Joe's knee has received what was needed in this session. At that point, I would ask Joe how his knee is feeling. Usually, Joe would indicate some improvement. His knee might not be completely healed yet, but improvement is certainly what we're going for. It's likely he would need more than one session if it's not better. Remember, the longer Joe has had his knee issue, the more sessions he may need to reverse the process back to completely well. If he just strained his knee, he might receive dramatic improvement from one session. Also, the energy will continue to work on him after our session is complete. He may feel even better later in the day.

The point is, by paying attention, I can tell when his knee has received what it's going to receive in this session. If my hands were over Joe's shoulders, I might be less inclined to sense the change in the flow of energy around his knee. Plus, remember I was not "putting" the energy on

Joe's knee. I was only noticing that his knee was receiving energy, and noticing when it had received enough during this session. If I were to move my hands to Joe's heart chakra while his knee was still receiving energy, I would sense how strongly the Reiki was being received in his heart chakra. *But energy would still be flowing to Joe's knee if I did this!* Moving my hands only moves my attention – not the Reiki!

It's very important to remember that the energy goes where it's needed and the person is ready to receive it. You are not putting the energy anywhere with your hands. If the person responds to your hands, saying the energy coming from your hands feels warm, that is because the person is paying attention to her own body where your hands are. It's natural to do this. But it doesn't mean that your hands are putting the energy there. The energy is flowing to all places that have a need, not just where your hands are located at any given moment. The recipient may be more sensitive to her own body where your hands are hovering due to her paying attention to that body part. If her eyes were closed, she would likely feel energy in many different places, regardless of where your hands were.

Reiki for objects, plants and animals

You can also charge any object, food, or liquid with Reiki energy. To do so, simply connect with the Reiki by saying or thinking "Reiki." Then, hold or hover your hands over the object you are intending to charge with Reiki energy for three to five minutes. Whatever object you charge with Reiki energy will give off a steady flow of Reiki in its area or to whoever holds it. Food and water will become purer and more balanced on a molecular level. (For a fascinating study of the effects of intention on water, refer to the work of Masaru Emotu, *Messages from Water*.)

Plants and animals also benefit from Reiki energy. Offer Reiki to your pets and see how they react. Spend a few minutes giving Reiki to a plant or a tree. I've had students report plants growing flowers off-season, cats recovering quickly from illness, and even fish recovering from injuries after receiving Reiki. Offering Reiki to your pets and plants is great practice for you, and a wonderful way to bond with the living things in your life.

Situation/Qualities Healing

This is the most important concept to understand about Reiki because the Situation/Qualities healing is the wild card, fill-in-the-blank healing. It is the one for which **you define the intention**. For example, you might intend "relieve pain," or "release stress," or "open opportunities for abundance," or any million things that you can dream up that you want the energy to do! In fact, **all Reiki healings are Situation/Qualities healings because they are all intentions!** I put that in bold to emphasize it! Everything, including turning the Reiki on, is an expression of **intention!** You intend to connect with Reiki. You intend what the energy should do. Whatever it is, it's an intention. You could simply be attuned to Reiki and then be turned loose to come up with your own intentions every time! But Practical Reiki gives you a good list of intentions (defined in each level) that you can immediately use instead of making you think up all of them yourself. The Situation/Qualities healing shows you that **you have the power** with your intention to define what you want the Reiki to do. So if something hurts you, intend for that something to receive pain relief. If you are trying to get over something from your past, send healing to that moment when the event transpired. The limits are only those which **you** set! Are you feeling the power of this yet?

It's a good practice to learn to set positive intentions. Word your intentions in a positive way, such as "relieve pain" rather than "send Reiki to Jessie's headache." Don't worry if you say it the second way, though. You won't be strengthening Jessie's headache with Reiki. The **intention** behind your words is to make his headache better. But still, the more you use a positive wording, the more you get used to doing that in your life in general, and that in itself can have positive effects on your life.

Remember that the energy will only be received as the recipient (including yourself) is ready and willing to receive. So you can't hurt anyone with Reiki because the person receiving is ultimately in charge of receiving (or blocking) anything that's not for his or her highest good. Isn't that a relief?

That isn't to say that energy cannot be negative. There is plenty of negative energy out there (and in our thoughts!). But Reiki energy is not negative. It is life force energy itself. That's why we need Reiki. Reiki will clear the negative out so we are in balance again. You can also intend Reiki for protection. Remember, you can set any intention with the Situation/Qualities healing.

Distance healing

Reiki energy is not limited by physical proximity or time. If that sounds unbelievable to you, think of a cell phone. You can call anyone in the world who has a phone. Its signal carries a frequency immediately across a vast distance. Similarly, you can direct Reiki energy to be received by anyone, anywhere in the world. (Regardless of whether that person has a phone.) The fact that Reiki works over any distance validates the idea that we are all connected by this life force energy that runs through and all around all living things.

Reiki is sent and received by distance via intention. (I bet you knew I would say that). No picture of the person is necessary, and you don't need to already be acquainted with the person to whom you are sending Reiki. It helps to have the first and last name of the recipient, but even less information can work.

You may wonder how the energy "knows" who to go to once you have directed it. If José in Mexico asks me for a

Reiki healing, how will the energy know which José in Mexico should receive it? The answer is that the energy will go to the José who requested it from me, the same José to whom I am intending to send the Reiki.

If I don't know any of the names of the people, but I know something to specify direction with, that can work too. For example, if an ambulance is speeding by and I don't know who is in it, I can ask that Reiki energy be received by the person who needs healing in that ambulance, and his or her medical team, if they are willing to receive it. That's specific enough. Again, it's the intention that gets it there, and you can express that intention in names or descriptions. If you know in any way who you want the energy to go to, the energy will too. So "the person from the grocery store who asked me to send her Reiki today," "the miners trapped in Chile," and "Sally's cousin who is in the hospital" are all valid ways of describing the recipient of the distance Reiki you're offering.

In the energetic world, time is in the eternal present. Although we experience time as linear, because time is actually all one, energy can be in more than one place at the same time. Quantum Physics has verified this as fact. *(Look it up if you want to know more about that. Quantum Physics lessons are beyond the scope of this book.)*

In any case, Reiki energy can very effectively be directed to a person anywhere in the world, now or in the future, by intention.

It can be helpful, when circumstances allow, for you to ask for feedback from the person to whom you're sending distance healing. This is because 1) it's validating for you to know that it's working, and 2) asking for feedback lets the recipient know you care enough to want to know that he or she feels better once you've sent it.

Sometimes it won't be possible to get feedback, however. For example, if you hear on the news that an earthquake has hit Japan, you may want to just send Reiki healing to all the people of Japan who are affected by the earthquake. You won't be expecting anyone from Japan to call and thank you. Or if Aunt Matilda has been rushed to the hospital, you'll want to send her Reiki now, and not worry over whether she felt it or not. In those cases, you just send it, trusting that it will arrive and be received as needed.

There are three ways to send distance Reiki.

1. **In Real Time.** This means that I am sending Reiki healing to another person (or people), to be received now, at this moment. This can be referred to as "intend and send." First, you turn on the Reiki by thinking or saying "Reiki on." Then, you intend "Distance healing for (name)" and add any Situation/Qualities intention if there is one. Then you simply sit a few minutes with the energy flowing until you feel it is done. Usually, this will happen in 5-7 minutes.

   For example: I receive a call from my husband, who is at work and has a headache. He asks if I will send him Reiki to help relieve his headache. I intend "Reiki on. Healing for Evan Langholt, to relieve the pain of his headache," and then I sit quietly for a few minutes, feeling the Reiki flow to Evan. I hold my hands with my palms facing each other, because when I do this, I am placing my attention on my palms and the energy sensations I feel there. I know from the sensations in my palms that the Reiki is flowing to Evan, and also when it stops. The energy is starting and going to Evan right now, as I intend it to.

   The "Real Time" method is good for any time you are wanting to send Reiki now to be received now. It doesn't matter whether the recipient is paying attention or not, the Reiki is going to that person immediately when you are sending it.

2. **Preset.** This method is for when you want the Reiki energy to begin working at a predetermined date and time in the future, but you want to send it now. To do this, first, turn on the Reiki by intending "Reiki on." Then, intend "Distance Reiki for (name) to be received at (date, time)." If the person is in another time zone, you can add "in his/her time zone" to the instructions. Of course, if you have a situational intention to add, that can be added as well. See the examples below.

Example #1: my daughter, Rayna, has a math test that she's worried about (even though she studied), on Thursday at 1:00 pm. She asks me to send her Reiki on Thursday at 1:00. But I will be teaching at that time, so I can't send it to her in real time. I choose to preset the Reiki for her by sending it now, intended for her to receive it on Thursday at 1:00 pm. I intend, "Reiki on. Distance Reiki for Rayna, to be received on Thursday at 1:00 pm, for mental clarity and confidence." Then I sit quietly for a few minutes with my palms facing each other, feeling the energy flow. On Thursday, the Reiki will begin flowing for Rayna automatically at 1:00 pm as scheduled, without Rayna or me needing to do anything more. Think of the Preset Reiki method as setting a lamp on a timer device, so that it will turn on at a specific time automatically.

Example #2: You can also use the preset method for yourself. If I know that I have an important meeting on Monday morning at 9:00 am, I will preset Reiki to be received by me on Monday morning at 9:00 am. Or I might even start it flowing at 8:45 am so I don't walk into the meeting nervous! That way I don't have to remember to give myself Reiki at that time while I'm trying to remember whatever I'm supposed to talk about. It'll just be there for me, starting automatically, even if I forget that I had sent it to myself.

3. **Queued.** This method allows you to send Reiki ahead of time, and the energy will be received *when the recipient intends to receive it.* This needs to happen intentionally. I jokingly call it "DVR Reiki" because it's just like recording a healing ahead of time, and then when the person it was recorded for is ready, he presses the "play" button by intending for the Reiki to begin. The energy stays in the recipient's energy field until it is "called in" by the recipient intending "I am now receiving the Reiki sent by (your name)."

Truthfully, the recipient could simply say, "Reiki, GO!" or "I want my Reiki NOW!" and the Reiki would start at that moment. Why? Because they are all ways to express the **intention** to receive the Reiki healing, and intention is what matters! But, I like to make it a little more formal by telling the recipient to use a full sentence to intend to receive the energy. Also, it seems a little flip to have the person say "Reiki GO!" so he may not take it seriously and it could make him doubtful that it would work if he did.

Here's how queuing a Reiki healing is done: First, intend "Reiki on." Then, intend "Reiki healing for (name), queued for (him/her) to receive when (he/she) is ready." Then simply hold your palms facing each other and feel the energy flowing until it stops. Your part is done!

You'll want to give your recipient some directions on how to receive the Reiki. I usually give these instructions to the recipient: *"When you are ready to receive the energy, please rest in a quiet place, and intend once softly, 'I will now receive the healing sent by Alice.' The energy will begin immediately upon your intention to receive. Just gently tune in and receive the healing energy. The best way to describe the mindset is be an observer and just notice what's different for the next half hour or so. The session will last around 25 minutes. I recommend that you rest in a quiet place, undisturbed by phone or TV. Soft music is fine if you prefer it. There is no need to repeat the statement, meditate, concentrate, or otherwise. Just place a gentle awareness on your physical and emotional state to feel the energy working. It helps to close your eyes, because some people experience color changes or images with their eyes closed during a Reiki healing. If you fall asleep, you will still receive the healing, but won't be as aware of the experience (which is the fun part, I think)."*

I also give the recipient some information about how Reiki may feel: *"Reiki energy is a subjective experience. It may feel: warm, tingly, like waves of soothing feelings, make you feel "lighter" emotionally, relaxing, release pain, relieve stress, increase clarity, you may see colors, and/or have a strong sense of well being come over you. You may sense presences around you or have other sensations. It depends on the ways in which you are sensitive to energy."*

I love queuing a healing because I know that the recipient will be paying attention to how she feels during the session, and will be able to give me some feedback afterward about how the energy was experienced. Feedback can be very useful.

Scanning: an advanced technique - optional

Once you get comfortable giving Reiki healings, you may wish to try scanning, which is a technique used to get a sense of the places where energy is being received, where it's blocked, and where pain and issues may be located. The energy will communicate with you through your clairs. Here's how to scan. After intending for the Reiki to start, as it flows, slowly run one or both hands a few inches above the person you are treating, moving over each chakra location. (Here's where that chapter on chakras comes in handy.) As your hand moves, pay attention to the sensations you receive via your major clair. What changes? Where do you feel more or less energy flow? Everything is significant, even if it is subtle. As you note nuances in the flow of energy, pay attention to them. This attention will help you notice more. Each change in sensation can be thought of as the energy communicating a message to you.

It is possible to do remote scanning during any distance healing, whether real time, preset, or queued. When I do a distance healing, I will scan the recipient to determine where I noticed the energy is being received. I will provide some of these observations in an email when I notify the person that his or her Reiki is queued and ready to be received. It can be useful, validating, and interesting to compare where I noticed the energy being received with the feedback that the recipient provides after her Reiki session.

To scan during a distance healing, begin by defining an area in the space in front of you which will represent the person to whom you are sending Reiki. You're defining a doll-sized body shape for the person in the air in front of you—here's his head, here's his chest, arms, trunk, legs, etc. Your intention places the facsimile of the person's energy into that space for you to scan. Then, just intend that Reiki begin and scan the space as if that were the person. Pay attention to what you notice as you go along. Take note of places that grab your attention. You may wish to ask the recipient about those places later. For example, if you notice a big change in the energy flow as you scan the stomach area, you may ask him if he had a stomach ache.

When scanning by distance, you have the power to use your intention to define the space in any way you'd like. For example, you can "grow" the person huge so that you can focus on scanning a very small part of the person. For instance, if you want to just intend Reiki healing to focus on the left lung area, you can make the space in front of you represent the person's left lung, and scan it for areas which need healing.

Remember, you are not "putting" healing in any one place. When you are scanning, you are **noticing** where the energy is going based on the changes in sensations you experience when you focus on different parts of the person. You do not need to scan in order to do a good Reiki session. You can be as involved as you want to be as the energy flows. As long as you intended for the energy to flow to the person, it will do that. You can simply offer the energy, hold your hands in one position, and the energy will still go where the person is ready to receive it. Scanning just allows you to enter into the dialog and observe where the energy is being received.

Cleansing a Room

This involves cleansing the energy in a room to remove any negative energy. Negative energy can be present in a room due to many possible factors. An argument can leave energetic "residue" in the room. So can a person in a foul mood. If people have a bad day and come home, or into your office, and then talk about it (or just fume about it silently), the room can be left with some negative energy. Those are just some examples. With Practical Reiki, it's easy to clear the energy in a room. The effects can be noticed afterward too! I've had students tell me that after cleansing their office, people come in and are much more pleasant than before.

Cleansing a room is easy to do. First, connect with the energy by saying or thinking, "Reiki". You always do that first. The intention to connect with the Reiki energy is as important as turning on your radio before you begin pressing buttons. The buttons won't do anything unless it's on!

Next, intend "Cleansing a room," and then specify the room (or rooms – you could intend the whole house if you want to) that you wish the energy to cleanse. Then hold your hands with palms facing each other while you feel the energy flowing, for about five to seven minutes. That's it! It's recommended that you cleanse the energy in your home every two weeks or more often as needed. This can be done for your own space or any other space you designate. Try it on a home that is up for sale but not getting any interest. It may just make the space more inviting.

Karmic Band Healing

This is a relationship healing. It is for the cord that is the energetic representation of the relationship between two people. When a relationship becomes strained, the cord needs healing. The Karmic Band healing is for the purpose of healing and strengthening relationships of all kinds. It may also be done between a person who is living and one who has passed on, especially if there is a feeling of a lack of closure in the relationship. It can also be done on behalf of two people besides oneself. I have done Karmic Band healing between two of my kids who pick on each other often. You can also do Karmic Band healing between you and another person you are close with, simply to strengthen the bonds between you. You don't have to feel that something is "wrong" in order to activate Karmic Band healing.

The Karmic Band healing does not require permission to activate. This is because it is not a healing for any person directly, but instead goes to the energetic cord of one person's relationship with another. You don't even need to tell the person that you activated the healing on his or her behalf.

Here's how to do it. First, connect with the energy by saying or thinking, "Reiki." Then intend "Karmic Band healing between (first person's name) and (second person's name)." If it's yourself, then intend "between (person's name) and me." You've now set your intention, and all you need to do is to sit for five to seven minutes with the energy flowing. Sitting with your palms facing each other can help you focus on the sensation of the energy flowing, until you become aware of the session being finished. You will generally feel a sense of closure or completeness, or the sensation of the energy flowing will simply end or taper off.

I have had numerous students report to me with surprise that after activating the Karmic Band healing, the person they intended the healing for suddenly called them. One student reported that he was very skeptical it would do anything at all, but he did the healing anyway, as it was a requirement of practicing the healings for level 1. He activated the healing for the karmic band between his sister and himself, and also between an estranged friend and himself. Neither his sister, nor the old friend were speaking to him at the time. Not only that, but it had been years since he had spoken to either. Shortly after he activated the Karmic Band healing, his sister called his mother and told her that she wanted to reestablish a relationship with him. His friend also called and did the same. My student was stunned, and sheepishly acknowledged that this healing works, no matter how skeptical the practitioner is at the time of activating it.

Another student reported activating the Karmic Band healing between herself and a coworker. This coworker and her had been having a strained relationship due to some politics at work. After activating the healing, she and the coworker managed to be cordial with each other and work together well on a project. They didn't become best friends, but there were definite improvements in their relationship.

Why does the Karmic Band healing work? In one respect, you could see it as sending out positive healing energy for the desire to have a better relationship with the other person. In that way, the energy works on that intention. It is strengthened by the practitioner's desire to have a better relationship with such-and-such a person, so it helps send healing and good energy to that goal.

- **Important things to know before continuing to level 2:**

It is recommended that the student wait at least two full days between the level 1 and level 2 attunements. Longer is fine, although there is no need for many weeks in between. In fact, the more you can practice the level 1 healings daily, the sooner you'll be ready to move forward. **It is necessary to complete each level 1 healing at least once before moving on to level 2.** The amount of time it takes you to do this is up to you. Most of my students spend a week working with the level 1 healings before requesting the level 2 attunement.

It is also highly recommended that you begin a daily self-healing routine immediately following your first attunement. The level 1 practices give you experience, which strengthens your intuition. When you do them daily, you also receive validation that this works, which strengthens your confidence. The more you practice, the more these important healing methods become easy to recall and choose based on the situation towards which you wish to direct Reiki. So the benefits of practicing the level 1 healings are: strengthening intuition, increasing confidence, and creating familiarity with the methods of level 1. These are all important parts of learning Practical Reiki.

There are many, many ways to incorporate Reiki into your daily life. You can offer Reiki healing to your pets, plants, children, water, office, car, bedroom, and food. You can charge your pillow, child's stuffed animal, favorite necklace, stones, essential oils, lotions, bath water, and shower head with Reiki and enjoy the resulting benefits. Infants are easily soothed by Reiki. Children and adults alike sleep better when they receive Reiki before bedtime. Help children (or yourself) relax and get back to sleep after a nightmare by offering some Reiki. Send Reiki to the past to heal the effects of an upsetting event. Send Reiki to future events for all to go well. You set the parameters by your intention, and this list is by no means complete. Just remember to 1) connect with the Reiki, 2) set the intention, and 3) allow the energy to flow. Intend and send. It's that easy.

One of my students is fond of saying "Reiki changes things." This is a simple and profound truth about Reiki. The more you use it, the more you'll find it's true for you too.

6

PRACTICAL REIKI LEVEL 2

The Practical Reiki level 2 attunement brings in the Earth energy from below your feet, traveling up your legs, entering through the base/root chakra and body to meet the Reiki energy which comes into the crown chakra and flows downward. The two energy sources merge at the heart chakra. They strengthen and ground your energetic connection between the Earth and cosmos, giving you a stronger frequency of energy to direct with your intention. The root chakra is opened further to let this Earth energy in. These changes may or may not be sensed by you during your attunement. It really depends on how sensitive to energy you are. The level 2 attunement feels stronger to some, and more subtle to others, compared with the level 1 attunement. It's very individual. No matter how it feels, if you intend to receive it, and the Reiki Master attuning you intends to attune you, it works. That's the important part.

The Level 2 Attunement

This attunement will further strengthen your ability to sense and work with Reiki energy. This is due to the combination of regular practice and the addition of the Earth energy to the mix.

The Practical Reiki Cleansing

After your Practical Reiki level 2 attunement, there is only one additional healing practice to do. It's called the Practical Reiki Cleansing. The Practical Reiki Cleansing is a specific self healing which you activate daily for at least a week before you receive your level 3 attunement. It's also an excellent "maintenance" self healing for everyday use. This healing begins a cumulative cleansing of your entire energetic system. Each successive day you activate it allows it to do more healing work on you, continuing where it left off the time before. Giving yourself this healing daily for a week helps prepare you for the level 3 attunement.

Note: because the Practical Reiki Cleansing is only a self healing, you won't be using this as a healing for other people. If you want to offer chakra cleansing to another person, intend "Reiki," and then "cleanse and balance chakras" and add the person's name if it is a distance healing. In person, simply place or hover your hands over your intended recipient wherever comfortable.

Of course, it is important to continue working on the healings for level 1, not only throughout this level, but always. As mentioned in the previous chapter, level 1 isn't just for the first part of learning Reiki. It's the foundation of the method that you'll use most often in your Reiki practice now, years from now, and in between.

To activate the Practical Reiki Cleansing, first intend to connect with Reiki by saying or thinking "Reiki." Then, intend "Practical Reiki Cleansing," Place your hands on yourself wherever you'd like, as you would for self healing. Many of my students prefer to activate this healing as they go to sleep at night. It's very relaxing, may help you sleep, and it's perfectly ok to fall asleep after you activate it.

You only need to say or think "Practical Reiki Cleansing" because you know what this healing is meant to do. Therefore, the name "Practical Reiki Cleansing" contains and therefore represents the full definition of its intention. If you didn't know what this healing is supposed to do, it would not work for you. Your knowledge of the meaning has attached itself to the title of the healing, making the name into a symbol that activates the intention just by saying its name.

Some people like to do the Practical Reiki Cleansing first thing in the morning or during a quiet time during the day. It is fine to do this healing whenever it works for you. It's also okay to do it at a different time each day if that's what your schedule permits. If you want to do the healing more than once per day, that is also ok.

You may also do regular or Situation/Qualities self healing at another time during the day. Even if you have done a different self healing that day, still do the Practical Reiki Cleansing once daily. You cannot overdose on healing energy. The more you practice, the more you gain. Once you've received a certain amount of healing in a day, you may feel you've had all you need for that day. The energy will work until you have received enough for that day, and then it will stop.

The Practical Reiki Cleansing is a specific self healing, so you don't offer a Situation/Qualities modification to it. It has a purpose in its definition, and that is its intention. If you have pain in your hip, for example, use the basic self healing with a Situation/Qualities intention to relieve pain or heal the cause of your hip pain. Do this separately from the Practical Reiki Cleansing. Think of the Practical Reiki Cleansing as a good daily maintenance routine that has a specific function. General self healing goes where it's needed, but it may do other things separate from the chakra and meridian cleansing that the Practical Reiki Cleansing activates. So choose general self healing when you want something less specific, choose Situation/Qualities healing when you want something very specific, and choose Practical Reiki Cleansing when you want the daily chakra cleansing. Of course, as I mentioned before, be sure to activate the Practical Reiki Cleansing daily between levels 2 and 3.

If you miss doing the Practical Reiki Cleansing one day during the week, don't worry too much over it. If you miss two days during the week, add two days before your level 3 attunement so that you have at least seven days of receiving the Practical Reiki Cleansing before your third attunement. Seven days straight of the Practical Reiki Cleansing will make the attunement more effective because it doesn't need to wade through energetic blockages to do its work of attuning you to the strongest level of Practical Reiki in this system. Attunements are very healing, and they empower you with a stronger connection (perhaps a "wider bandwidth" of healing frequencies), plus the ability to more easily feel the energy working as a result. The more you have prepared yourself by "cleaning house" (meaning your own energy) before the attunement, the less healing the attunement will need to do for you. An analogy: you are paying a person who comes to your house and provides both cleaning and painting services. You have paid for two hours of this person's time. If your house is a mess, he will spend the bulk of those two hours cleaning, and get very little painting done. If you've already done a lot of cleaning yourself, he will be able to spend most of his time painting and making your house beautiful.

Think of this week of the Practical Reiki Cleansing as giving yourself the benefits of strong and thorough self healing and continued practice. It will make a very big difference in many ways.

7

PRACTICAL REIKI LEVEL 3 (MASTER)

Remember how level 1 was the "meat and potatoes" of Practical Reiki? Level 3 provides the tasty little side dishes. All of the healing methods in level 3 are different intentions for the energy. It would be completely possible for you to receive attunements to Practical Reiki and then be told to use your intention to direct the energy, without giving you much further instruction. In fact, if you think about it, every single healing you do with Reiki is a Situation/Qualities healing. That is because for everything you do with Reiki once you "turn on" the energy, you are using intention to give the instructions. So even self healing or "the healing that is needed" is an intention that tells the Reiki to do a general healing. So you could simply receive your attunements and be set free to direct the energy on your own from there.

But it can be difficult on your own to come up with all of the things that Reiki can do. So the healing methods throughout this text are suggested ways to direct the Reiki energy. Many of them, especially those in level 3, may be things you wouldn't have thought of on your own. Think of them as being the sample pictures that come with your new camera software. They're there to show you some possible ways to use your new camera. Learn them, and then go out and take pictures on your own. That's what you need to do with the healing methods in this system. Take them, learn them, practice them on yourself and others, and then create your own ways to incorporate them into your world. Do you feel powerful and free now? You should, because **you are!**

The Level 3 Attunement

The level 3 attunement further opens your chakras to allow for the strongest flow of the combined Earth energy and Reiki energy. By now, you have completed a week of the Practical Reiki Cleansing self healing and you're ready for the level 3 attunement which will complete your attunement process. This attunement does the important work of empowering you to attune others to Practical Reiki. It is a Master level attunement. Therefore, after receiving the attunement, you are qualified to call yourself a Practical Reiki ™ Master. When you attune and teach another person, you will be a Practical Reiki™ Master Teacher. (Refer to the introduction for a reminder of the meaning of this title.)

For this level, it is important that you complete **all** of the healings listed on yourself the requisite number of times before doing **any** of them on another person, or attuning another person to Practical Reiki. Each healing session with the methods of level 3 can be given in five to 15 minutes. You may continue to practice any of the healing methods from level 1 as usual while you are proceeding through the series of level 3 healings on yourself.

There are several important reasons for this. They are:

1. In order to give yourself the healings from level 3, you need to learn them. You need to understand what each is supposed to do in order for them to work on you. The name of the healing will only direct the energy if you know what that healing is meant to do—that is the intention behind that healing. The intention resides in your own understanding and thoughts. So intending the name of the healing will only direct the energy if you already understand what the healing is meant to do for you. In simple language, this means you have to **learn the meaning of the healings of level 3.**

2. You receive the benefits of each of the healings for level 3 by giving them to yourself. That's a lot of healing, and it's good for you! Establishing a practice of regular self healing is very important, and going through each of the healings for level 3 can help to get you into the habit of self care with

Reiki. To summarize: you will **receive the benefits of each of the healings of level 3.**

3. You experience each of the healings of level 3 by giving them to yourself. By paying attention to how each one feels, you both strengthen your own intuition by observing the differences, and you gain valuable experience that you can then use to help offer the healings to others. (I recommend that you make some notes after each self healing with the level 3 healings. Knowing you will be jotting down your experiences will help you pay attention, and the notes will be useful for you as a reference later.) In short: **your experience will help you be a better practitioner and (eventually) teacher.**

Once you've completed all of the level 3 healings on yourself, you have a full toolbox of energy healing techniques to choose from. Most importantly, you know what each tool is meant to do, because you've experienced using it on yourself, and you know how it felt when you did. That combination of knowledge and experience will empower you to make the best choices when offering a healing to others, and also help you teach this method, should you decide to do that someday.

I have made it a practice not to award certificates of completion to students until they have completed the series of level 3 healings on themselves. I believe you really haven't completed your training until you have done the work of fully learning level 3, which includes these self healing practices. In adopting this requirement, I'm emphasizing the importance of mindful regular practice and modeling it for my students. It is my hope that my students will do the same when they become teachers of Practical Reiki.

The level 3 healings and how to activate them:

As with any Practical Reiki healing (except those only intended for self healing, i.e. self healing, the Practical Reiki Cleansing, and Balance), these healings may be given either in person or via distance. I recommend that you complete the healings for yourself in the order in which they are presented here. That way you won't lose track of which you've completed and which you still need to do.

Take special note of the healings that need to be done in two or more sessions to be complete. Others should be applied as needed.

For self healing, simply intend "Reiki" to activate the energy, and then say or think the name of the healing you intend to receive. Then place your hands on yourself wherever you are comfortable and let the energy flow until it's done.

Example: "Reiki, Causal Healing." then place your hands on yourself and relax, sensing the flow of the energy as it works until it's done.

<u>For another person,</u> intend "Reiki" to activate the energy, and then say or think the name of the healing you intend to offer.

- In person, place or hover your hands on the person you are treating. Choose where to put your hands based on where you both are comfortable. Gently observe the sensations of the energy flowing until it stops.

- By distance, intend "Reiki" to activate the energy, and then the name of the healing you intend to offer, followed by "for (name of person)." Queue, preset, or send in real time as described in chapter five. Hold your hands with palms facing each other and observe the sensations of the energy flowing until it stops.

Causal Healing

This healing sends energy to the underlying cause of an issue. Sometimes we don't know the reasons why we have certain problems or conditions. These triggers lie beneath the surface. They could be anything left over from childhood experiences, or unresolved feelings from any time in life. Sometimes we just feel "off" but aren't sure why we feel that way. This healing works on the deeper underlying cause of the problem or imbalance.

Crystalline Healing

Whenever we experience a physical or emotional trauma, a "crystal" forms in our energy. It's an energetic remnant of the experience. This is known as "muscle memory" in massage therapy. These crystals can cause ongoing physical pain, such as a recurring ache long after the physical injury, or emotional "baggage" that becomes triggered by an event that becomes a reminder of that hurt from the past. For instance, a skiing injury from two seasons ago still produces a sore knee from time to time. Another example: feeling angry long after the event that caused it was over, because you heard a person's name that sounds like the name of the person who was involved in the event. These crystals can be dissolved and released by this healing.

Note: Crystalline Healing needs to be given in two healing sessions. Each session gives half of the full healing. It is recommended that the sessions be given at least a day apart, or longer if the recipient feels more time is needed.

DNA Healing

Activating this sends healing energy deep into the DNA strands, our blueprint for life. The intention acts to repair any strands which are damaged due to genetics, diseases, or from environmental causes. Results may take time to notice, if at all, but all one needs to do is to be open to allowing the energy to work as intended.

For most people, only one DNA Healing session is necessary. However, if someone has a known genetic defect or inherited genetic problem, this healing may be repeated every three weeks.

Birth Trauma Healing

This healing is for the trauma of being born (not to be confused with the trauma of **giving birth**, which one should use a Situation/Qualities healing to address if needed). Although most of us don't remember this personally, being born is an intense experience which can create lasting emotional and physical memories in our energy system. This healing sends Reiki to gently release and heal any trauma which happened from our own birth experience. Only one Birth Trauma Healing per person is usually needed, unless someone has had an unusually difficult birth and you sense that a second session would be beneficial. (It is not possible to "overdose" on Reiki – if you offer healing that is not needed, the energy will simply not be received there. Remember the driveway and pothole analogy from chapter 1.)

Location Healing

Just as there are karmic bands between people, there are also relationship cords between people and places. Think of a place you were when something upsetting happened to you. Then think of every time you were in that place afterward. Did being there trigger memories of the upsetting situation? Did you feel unusually tense or upset again just from stepping foot into that place again? A Location Healing can work to heal and release the tie between that location, the event, and you.

This healing will work to heal and release all karmic location ties from your past experiences at once. You don't have to direct it towards any specific location or incident to activate it. However, if something happens to you that you wish to specifically request Location Healing for, you may simply intend Location Healing and then mention that specific place in your thoughts or softly aloud.

Past Life Healing

This healing works to release and heal residual blockages or traumas caused by one's past life experiences. While some past life experiences may be a part of your life's lessons in this lifetime, this healing may help 1) release those which you do not need to carry forward, and 2) make your lessons gentler and easier to accomplish.

Note: A complete Past Life Healing treatment requires three sessions. It is recommended that the sessions be given at least a day apart.

Also, some people report intense dreams after receiving a Past Life Healing session. If intense dreams continue after the third session has been given, it is advised to repeat the series of three sessions. Intense dreams are an indication of clearing, so think of this as letting the water run until it runs clear after the pipes have been flushed. Repeated instances of intense dreams simply means that the clearing is still happening. So it makes sense to continue the healing sessions until things return to normal.

Balance

This is a favorite of most of my students! Balance is the fastest healing to activate, and it only functions as a self healing. It will set in motion a healing that balances all of your chakras. The energy session continues for a full hour, just as if you were receiving an hour-long Reiki session. The effects last much longer! For some, this means a few days. For others, it could be shorter. The best thing about it is that it takes *only 30 seconds* to activate, and then you can go about your day.

To activate Balance, there is a specific hand position to use. Hold your hands with palms facing each other and firmly (but not hard) press each fingertip to its opposite on the other hand. For example, your left index fingertip presses against your right index fingertip, left middle fingertip to right middle fingertip, left ring finger to right ring finger, left pinky to right pinky, and left thumb to right thumb. Only the pads of the fingers touch each other, not the whole palm or whole finger. Your hands can be upright in front of you, resting on your lap, or any other way you wish to hold them as long as your fingers and thumbs are pressed together as described for the 30 seconds.

When you do this, intend "Balance" once softly or in thoughts. Hold the hand position for 30 seconds to activate this hour-long healing process. After the 30 seconds have passed, you may go about your day. The energy will actively work on your system for an hour.

This is an excellent healing to grab when you're feeling stressed out at any time. It's also well loved because it's so unobtrusive and doesn't draw any attention to you if you're doing the healing for yourself during a meeting or in a public place. It's a very common hand position for people to naturally assume. I've had students report great results from using this healing during tense times in a hospital waiting room, before or during an interview, in traffic, or any time when they feel stress coming on. (If you're driving, please wait until you're at a traffic light to take both hands off the wheel!)

Since it actively works on you for a full hour, it isn't necessary to activate it more than once per hour. Note: If you wanted to activate a chakra balancing healing for another person, just use the Situation/Qualities healing and intend "Balance chakras" after activating Reiki. Do not use the Balance hand position for another person. The hand position is only to enforce the intention for the self healing.

Important things to know about level 3:

The healings of level 3 are not all you can do with Practical Reiki, but they represent some powerful intentions that can inspire you to create your own ways to intend for healing to occur. Remember that the power is in the intention that you express. So you can combine healing intentions, send Reiki to one, two, ten, a hundred, a country's population, or the world if you wish. You can give a boost of Reiki to your pet, plant, food, room, home, car, office, bed, pillow, necklace, favorite stone, or glass of wine if you want, or anything else you can think of. The limits are those you define by your intention.

If you get one big message from this entire book, I hope it is this one: The three things that matter most when working with energy are: **intention, intention, intention!**

8

GIVING ATTUNEMENTS

Once you've completed the level 3 series of healings on yourself, you are empowered to teach and attune others to Practical Reiki The attunement procedure itself is very simple. I advise that if you will be attuning others to Practical Reiki, you teach them the method well. Make sure your students have a copy of this book as a textbook and you become a resource to answer their questions and guide them in addition to passing on the attunements. This powerful Reiki method deserves empowered and confident teachers who can bring others to become empowered and confident as well. Think of all of the people who could be out there sharing this healing energy. If you teach people well, they will do the same for those they teach. Think of the amazing positive changes we're bringing to the world together.

Here is your guide to passing on attunements.

The two most essential ingredients for successful attunements are:
1) The Reiki Master's intention to attune the recipient
2) The recipient's intention to receive the attunement.

Both need to be active for an attunement to work. The good news is that they don't need to be active at the same time. The attunement can be queued for the recipient to receive when ready, just as a distance healing can be queued. *Note: In the case of queued attunements, the attunement must be sent before it is received.* I will attest that distance attunements are equally as effective as in person attunements. I have attuned hundreds of people by distance and in person. This attunement procedure works either way.

Prepare your student(s) ahead of time:

Instruct your recipient(s) to sit, recline, or lie down comfortably in a quiet place, with hands resting palms-up. The recipient(s) should then intend once in thoughts to receive the Practical Reiki level (number) attunement. Instruct your recipient(s) to then simply place a gentle awareness on how they feel, and observe all sensations with a sense of wonder. No effort is needed. Just "be in the moment." Suggest that the recipient(s) have eyes closed until the attunement comes to an end. *Note: in a classroom situation, this is useful for knowing when all students' attunements have finished. When everyone's eyes are open, you can start to ask them to describe their attunement experience.*

After the attunement, whether in person or by distance, it is a good idea to ask the recipient(s) for feedback. This lets you know that the attunement was felt, shows the student that you care, and also gives students a chance to hear each other's experiences. This validates the idea that everyone's experience is different, but everyone feels *something*.

Giving a Practical Reiki attunement:

1) Ask for protection and assistance from your guides, angels, Spirit, Master Kuthumi (see Appendix B), and/or any deity/Higher Beings you feel connected with on a spiritual level. This step is a mindful way of acknowledging that we are part of the energy of All That Is, however you see it. Reiki is not a religion, but it is a spiritual practice. *(Note: If you are not comfortable with this step, you may omit it. You can add it in if your comfort level changes. The attunement will work either way. I did not include this step for a long time in my own practice. Once I did decide to try it, I felt more supported, so I've kept it as part of my own practice, which I feel has been strengthened because of it.)*

2) Connect with the Reiki energy by intending "Reiki" and pause for 20-30 seconds until you feel the energy flowing strongly. I hold my hands up when I

do this. Holding my hands up briefly during this step has become my physical gesture of intention to connect with Reiki. It would still work if I didn't hold my hands up, but doing so helps me to strongly define my intention, so I like to do it this way.

3) When you feel the energy flowing strongly, intend "Life force energy will be generated and will not fade until this attunement is complete." This is the beginning of the actual attunement procedure.

4) Intend "Practical Reiki level (number) attunement for (name)." This sets the intention to attune the recipient. If there is more than one recipient, simply say or think each person's name. If the attunement is to be queued, add "queued for him/her to receive when he/she is ready."

5) Ask for assistance from the recipient's Higher Self in receiving this attunement, and add an intention for the recipient to be fully empowered to use Practical Reiki level (number) when the attunement is complete. You can use your own words here. I usually say or think, "I ask for assistance from (name)'s Higher Self in attuning (name) to Practical Reiki level (number). May (name) be fully empowered to use Practical Reiki in a confident and successful way after receiving this attunement. Thank you."

6) If you are with the person you are attuning, place your hands lightly on your recipient's shoulders for about 20 seconds. This establishes rapport and tends to strengthen the sensations of the attunement process for the recipient as well. (If you are attuning a class, do this for each student individually. If you are attuning by distance, omit this step.)

7) Sit quietly for 5-10 minutes with palms facing each other, feeling the energy flow. You don't need to concentrate or meditate; just be mindfully present. If you are with the person(s) you are attuning, wait quietly for the person(s) to open his or her eyes to signify being finished.

8) Ask the recipient(s) to talk about the experience. Remind and encourage the recipient(s) to follow up with the practices associated with this attunement level. Plan a time to touch base with the student(s) about how practices are going, and to schedule the next attunement (if applicable).

Tips:

- Be sure your student(s) know about grounding and how to handle possible clearing symptoms.
- Remind your student(s) that practice will strengthen the sensations of the energy and make them consistent.

- Encourage your student(s) to ask for feedback from those to whom they offer Reiki.
- Trust that if you intended to attune the student, and the student intended to receive the attunement, that all went as it should. Have quiet confidence in yourself and the power of intention.

9

IMPORTANT CONSIDERATIONS FOR ALL
WHO PRACTICE REIKI

Congratulations! You are empowered with Reiki! You are a super hero of healing! But wait a moment. Before you go out and heal the world, there are some ethical and practical issues of importance of which you should be aware.

The ethics of permission

Just as you wouldn't want a doctor to force you to take a certain medicine, you wouldn't want to force healing on anyone. Everyone has the free will to refuse or accept a Reiki healing. No matter how tempted you are to just send Reiki to someone who you believe needs it, you shouldn't assume the person wants it. People have their own reasons for wanting or not wanting a certain treatment, whether it is conventional or "alternative" therapy. Some people have religious reasons to refuse energy healing. Others are afraid or not ready to be open to receiving Reiki. The first priority, therefore, is to ask for and receive permission to give or send Reiki energy to whomever you are intending to treat.

At first, this idea may seem silly. It's healing energy! It's good! Everyone should want it! I'm not even touching the person! How could it hurt? But remember: **giving Reiki is doing something.** Because it is real, it matters enough to take it seriously.

In order to get some perspective on this issue, try to put yourself on the other side for a moment. Imagine that you do not know about Reiki. You are at work and are not feeling well. A coworker who you don't know well decides to send some energy to you by distance without letting you know it's coming. Suddenly, you feel strange. There's a heat coursing through you. You feel a little light-headed. You decide you must have a fever and go straight to the doctor because you don't understand these new sensations, instead of going home to rest. If your well-meaning coworker would have taken the time to ask you first, you could have decided whether you wanted to try this healing method. You would have been informed that there could be some new sensations (heat or light-headedness) associated with this energy, so you wouldn't have been alarmed. You might also have been in the right mindset to notice that your original symptoms were relieved, and the ungrounded feeling could be resolved quickly and easily (if only your coworker would have told you how to ground your energy).

Here's another scenario. Your friend's brother, Joe, is having ongoing pain from his recent surgery. You decide to send Joe some Reiki, but don't ask him first. He feels better more quickly than expected, without knowing why. He just assumes that he's a fast healer. Alternatively, you have your friend ask Joe if he would be receptive to you sending some Reiki energy his way to help him with pain relief and healing. Joe is skeptical but agrees. To his surprise, he feels much better. Joe gets in touch with you and you tell him more about Reiki. He tells his doctor about it, decides to continue receiving Reiki, and eventually learns it for himself. He starts offering Reiki to others and talks about how much it has helped him. Because you chose to ask his permission first, there is now another Reiki practitioner in the world sharing healing with others.

And here is a very important example to further illustrate the point about permission. For children (not your own), you need to get permission of the parent or guardian before offering Reiki. **It can be very tempting to ignore this rule!** This is especially true if the child is in your classroom and you are the teacher! Suppose your student comes into class with a headache. Unless you were hired to teach Reiki, you may not offer Reiki just as you may not give the child an over-the-counter pain reliever without parental consent.

Here's a little story that happened to me when I was new to Reiki and excited about being able to help people with this wonderful energy. I was teaching sixth grade in a Sunday School class. One of my students came into class complaining of a headache. I felt sympathy for him and wanted to help. I told him that I might be able to help him feel better. He asked if I had an aspirin, and I said no, but I could offer some energy with my hands by holding them over his head and it might help. The other kids giggled, but he agreed, and I intended Reiki in my thoughts and hovered my hands over his head. I continued to teach my lesson while I had my hands there. After about five minutes, I asked him how he felt. Surprised, he said, "My headache is gone!" I felt triumphant.

I went home and called my Reiki teacher and told her excitedly about helping the student with the headache. To my surprise, she admonished me. "You shouldn't have done that," she said. Taken aback, and a little defensive, I asked her why. She explained that maybe he had a headache because he was coming down with a virus. So I gave him Reiki and his headache went away for now. Suppose he goes home after Sunday School and tells his parents about how his teacher put this energy on his head when he had a headache. Then, that night, he gets sick because he was coming down with a virus anyway and the effects of the short Reiki healing wore off. His parents will think that something weird that the Sunday School teacher did made their kid sick. They'll call the principal the next day and angrily demand to know what kind of strange stuff is going on in that classroom, and who said the teacher could do that to their kid. Boom. I'm in trouble. Needless to say, I didn't sleep well that night. In doing something I thought was nice, I had crossed a line. (Things didn't play out that way, but they could have.)

"Stealth healing" is really not recommended as an ethical practice. Also, for pets that are not your own, you should get permission of the pet's owner before offering Reiki to his or her pet.

Now, there will be times when you just can't get permission. For example, if the intended recipient is in a coma, in surgery, or if you want to send Reiki to the victims of some disaster you heard about on the news. In those cases, err on the side of helping. Send anyway.

There is a "cover your butt" method to get around the permission issue. *This should not be used for your first choice, but only when permission is not possible to obtain.* Here's what you do: When you are setting your intention, ask for Reiki to go to the intended recipient **if his/her Higher Self is willing to receive it**, and if not, that it go to (the Earth, the Universe, etc.). That way, the decision is out of your hands, and you can't mess it up by assuming that someone wants Reiki.

Some practitioners I know say that they ask the intended recipient's Higher Self in their thoughts for permission, and tune in intuitively to sense an answer. I do not recommend this method to you or my students, because I think in many cases, it would be natural to "sense" that of course the person says "yes" because I believe they should. The asker's intuition will be skewed by what the ego wants to do. Some people are intuitive enough to get by with this method, but some are not. I don't trust myself to get a clear answer, due to my own strong desire to help, so I use the method above instead. I also think you can't go wrong with that method because you take your own desires out of the equation.

Confidentiality

As you work with Reiki you will become more sensitive to the nuances in the energy as it's flowing. Your intuition may alert you to places that are blocked in your client's energy. You may receive claircognitive messages about your client's situation. You will need to use discretion about what you communicate to your client. You don't have to tell everything you feel, especially if it may upset your client. You will also need to adopt a policy of confidentiality with your client. Don't share information about your sessions with other practitioners, family or friends, unless it is done so anonymously. And **never, ever diagnose** or suggest a course of treatment beyond Reiki unless you are a licensed health professional. You can suggest that the client follow up with his or her doctor if you sense something that needs attention. You can also ask your client questions relating to what you observe, to assess if your intuition is giving you useful information. These are essential ethical issues for anyone working with Reiki or intuition in any way.

Energetic Protection

As we work with intuition and energy, changes happen. The intuition grows stronger, and we become more sensitive to the energy that we work with, and the energy around us. For many, empathic senses get stronger. As we work with energy, our own energetic frequency, or "vibration" increases to a higher level. We become more tuned in to the information flowing into our crown and third eye chakras. All of these things are naturally occurring developments from mindful regular Reiki practice.

So when these changes happen—intuition is stronger, energetic frequencies are raised—we also become more sensitive to negative energy. We're like magnets that have grown stronger, and attract more of the opposite polarity that's around. Darkness is attracted to light. Negative energy is attracted to positive. So while practicing Reiki does not mean that we will absorb our client's negative energy, it does mean that we will become more sensitive to energy around us. Therefore, it's a good idea to learn and practice energetic protection techniques.

There are many ways to simply and quickly protect your energy before a Reiki session, before going into a crowded place, or any time you might feel vulnerable to negative energy. Even being around an angry or miserable person can make you feel drained. Energetic protection techniques can also help protect you from this result.

The quickest and most effective way to protect your energy is to **ground**. Refer to the grounding tree meditation and other techniques from chapter 5 for techniques to ground your energy.

You may also simply **ask** your guides, angels, or Spirit (in any form that feels comfortable to you) for protection at any time. I do this before starting a Reiki session or attunement for another person, or when I feel uncomfortable.

You can **envision yourself encased in a shield** of white or gold light that surrounds your entire aura, and intend that only positive energy can come in. Your intention is very powerful. Intending that your protective shield be active will work.

Try all of these techniques and get into the habit of grounding your energy daily. Grounding has many benefits besides energetic protection, including: increasing mental clarity, reducing stress, helping you feel calmer, and strengthening intuition.

Walk your talk

As Reiki practitioners, it can be easy to offer Reiki to everyone we can and neglect ourselves. Daily self healing should become the norm for us all. At the very least, as you lie down to go to sleep every night, activate a Reiki self healing. It's fine to fall asleep with the energy flowing. Also, don't forget to use Balance during the day whenever you need it. Keeping your energy clear and flowing each day will have health benefits that you will notice over time. The more you incorporate Reiki practice into your daily life, the more you'll see the results happen.

May your practice of Reiki help you live your best life and help you make the world a better place.

10

FREQUENTLY ASKED QUESTIONS

Will Reiki continue to flow if I get up and do
something else after I begin a session?

Yes. Reiki only needs you to intend to connect with the
energy and express your intention for it to flow per your
directions. If you do those two basic things, it will continue
for a short while longer, even if you get up and leave.
However, if you intend "stop," the Reiki will stop. So in
essence, an intentional "connect and push" is enough to at
least send a burst of healing energy toward your intended
goal. This sort of session won't last as long as one in which
you are fully engaged, but it will make a difference when
you are unable to sit mindfully for the full session.

Do I need my hands to send Reiki by distance?

No. You can send Reiki with your thoughts, provided you express the intention clearly in your thoughts or aloud at the beginning. However, I only choose this option when I absolutely can't sit for five to 10 minutes and feel the Reiki flowing.

Does Reiki work if I can't feel it? What if the person I'm attuning/treating can't feel it?

Yes. Whether you are a practitioner who is still learning to sense the subtle sensations of the energy, or a person who is receiving a Reiki healing, once a person is attuned to Reiki, the Reiki energy is flowing.

It can be hard to believe in something you can't feel though, so this can be difficult. I don't want people to have to take me "on faith" and just believe rather than experience the energy. I believe that experience is our best teacher of our truth. If you feel it, it's real for you. If you've experienced it, you have a frame of reference.

There can be many reasons why a person might not be aware of feeling the energy. Here are some of them:

- fatigue

- inexperience (not knowing what to expect to feel)

- over-thinking or over-analyzing each sensation

- health or emotional state which could mask the subtle energy sensations

- being hot, cold, or in pain which could cause the body to just register those physical sensations overwhelming energetic ones (unless the energy is causing the pain to subside, in which case it could be recognized).

- energetic blockages which need to be solved to process energetic sensations

- need for energy – maybe the person has had Reiki recently and doesn't need much at this moment

- denial – people who think that Reiki is fake, and are determined to believe it will have a harder time recognizing it if they would allow someone to offer them a healing.

It's also important to note that individuals are naturally sensitive to energy in their own way, which could be not at all, or could be involving natural psychic abilities. In short…everyone's different.

Another thing is everyone needs to become aware of his or her unique way of sensing energetic information. Usually these energetic sensitivities, called **clairs**, will fall into one of four categories: visual, hearing, touch, and knowing.

If you're visually sensitive, you may see colors, patterns, or images with your eyes closed.

If you're audiently sensitive, you may hear music, ringing, buzzing, or vibration in your ears.

If you're touch-sensitive, you may feel changes in temperature, tingles, waves of a magnetic or static-like feeling, pressure, lightness, or other physical responses.

And if you're cognitively sensitive, you may just "know" that something is different.

Becoming aware of your way of sensing intuitive information will help you pay attention to those particular sensations and recognize them when they happen. Your attention will also make them feel stronger and more nuanced as you practice or just tune in. So I always try to teach my students and clients to "be aware of your clair." (Refer to chapter 3 for more information on clairs).

If you just don't feel, see, hear, or sense anything, cut yourself some slack. If you're a practitioner, practice more. Also, get feedback from those to whom you offer energy. Do they feel it? What do they feel when you are giving them Reiki? Let that be reassuring to you.

The more you practice, the more you'll start to sense some patterns in the way you feel when giving Reiki. You may start to recognize a consistency and that is the energy talking to you.

If you are receiving Reiki and you don't feel or notice anything, place your awareness on how you feel in general before and afterward instead. What changes for you after you have your treatment? Do you notice less stress? Less pain? A more clear and positive feeling? Feel emotionally lighter? Results are more important than anything, really. Reiki is here to help you get into balance. Feeling the energy isn't really the goal of a Reiki healing.

How can I deal with people who say that Reiki is fake?

It depends. Some people will reserve judgment until they give you a chance to let them experience Reiki. They will ask intelligent yet skeptical questions and honestly allow themselves to experience Reiki before they decide. Those are not the people this question is addressing. Skepticism is fine—it implies that someone is open to trying the experience before making a decision about whether it is "True."

This question is meant to address those who flat out decide, and then proclaim, that Reiki is fake. They are closed-minded, having made their decision based on something other than experience. That could mean fear of the unknown, extreme religious doctrine, or being afraid to accept that there is more than their current version of reality. You have no chance to change their mind; they are looking for a chance to convince **you** that you are wasting your time.

But you know better, don't you? So how do you deal with these people?

The answer: you don't.

Do not defend yourself. Do not try to explain or prove that Reiki is powerful, helpful, healing, etc. You won't get anywhere.

Here's what you should do instead:

Keep practicing with **quiet confidence**. Ignore those who would try to put you down or invalidate your work.

One or both of these two things will happen as a result:

1) You will continue to serve those who need and benefit from Reiki. (This is your purpose, right?)

2) The naysayer will either notice your positive results, or he will continue to deny Reiki. Either way, you are still doing your part to make the world better and getting the positive results that validate this work for those who matter - you and those you serve. (See 1 above).

Is Reiki against religion?

No. Reiki is not a religion or a religious practice. It is a spiritual practice. If your religious leaders speak out against Reiki, they may not understand what Reiki is really about. Or they may be coming from a place of fear of the unknown, thinking that something that is not defined in their religious literature must be "wrong." You can't change someone's mind if they have that view.

However, I will tell you what I believe, along with many others I know who practice Reiki. We come from a wide variety of religious (and non-religious) backgrounds and beliefs.

I believe that life force energy exists in all living beings. This is the same energy that Reiki is at its essence. When I am offering Reiki to another person, I am offering that person more of what they, themselves, are made of, and are lacking in some places (which creates imbalance in those areas).

In addition, the person receiving Reiki is in charge (consciously or subconsciously) of exactly how much energy is received, and where it goes. I am simply offering energy to that person for that person to take, as one might offer a jar of lotion to someone who may then take some and apply it where needed.

If Reiki energy is the same life-energy that we have as part of us from conception, it is what we have been given by our Creator, however you choose to define that Source. Therefore, offering some of the same, which doesn't come from me, but instead through me, is just more of a universal redistribution of the same Source energy that's part of All That Is.

Prayer is another way of intending that energy move and change someone's situation. Asking for help from Source is pretty similar to asking that energy re-balance a person where needed. Reiki is not prayer, but there are parallels. If prayer is not against religion, neither is Reiki.

Is knowing your Reiki lineage important to being a legitimate Reiki practitioner?

First, here's what lineage is: Lineage is the link between the practitioner and the founder of Usui Reiki, Mikao Usui. The line of people between the practitioner and Sensei Usui is the lineage.

One of the reasons that some people believe lineage is important is to ensure someone has been trained by an "official" Reiki Master. The Reiki energy has been transferred person by person dating back to the original founder of Reiki, Mikao Usui himself.

For each of us, there are certain energetic frequencies that we carry naturally. Then there are those we've added as we've learned how to tap into our intuitive abilities. Perhaps some of us have learned meditation, perhaps yoga, perhaps some other forms of energy healing such as Quantum Touch, Polarity Therapy, Qi Gong, or Theta Healing. Each time we strengthen our intuition in any way, our vibration alters a little. So my Reiki energy may feel different from someone else's, even if we both learned the same Reiki method(s).

Think of it this way: You and I both learn to play a simple Mozart minuet on the piano. We spend the same amount of time practicing, with the same teacher. We both master the piece. Then, you and I each play it. Will there be differences? Yes, there will. It has the same notes, the same rhythm, we had the same teacher, and both practiced. What's different is the interpretation that we naturally give the piece as we play it. Subtle pressures yielding different dynamics, tones, and the mood created by the full interaction of each will be different because you and I are different. It's the same with Reiki.

This has to do with lineage in the way that if I learned Reiki from x teacher who learned it from Usui himself, and you learned it from y teacher, who learned it from a line ten people down from Usui, we are both channeling energy, and it won't be "watered down" but instead filtered through our own intuitive frequencies to get to the recipient.

The factors which influence the strength of the energy that the recipient is offered are more part of the practice of the person giving the healing. Here's what matters most:

- personal self healing
- dedicated, daily practice
- self reflection
- striving to improve one's life, health, and intuition
- giving and receiving Reiki regularly

This is what matters. If you were taught well by a dedicated teacher, and you practice mindfully and regularly, you will have strong, beautiful Reiki energy flowing through you. This is what makes you a "legitimate" Reiki practitioner.

Can Reiki be combined with other alternative therapies?

Yes! Reiki can complement and enhance the effectiveness of most any other method of healing you would choose. Whether you have (or give) a Reiki session in between treatments with the other method (e.g. massage, acupuncture, cranial-sacral work, polarity therapy, etc.), or the practitioner is incorporating Reiki into his or her work, Reiki can help!

Reiki energy balances the subtle frequencies of the person's energetic body as it is being received. So it can be combined with any other therapy to achieve deeper and more profound healing. Practical Reiki is so easy to activate, it can be combined with anything from a hug to a full massage. Just intend for the Reiki to flow as you practice your other techniques.

If I learn Reiki, and don't use it for a long time, will it stop working?

No. But if you stop working with the Reiki energy for a long period, when you start again, you may not feel the energy at first, or it might be very slight compared with the time when you were practicing regularly. That doesn't mean it has stopped working, it means you need practice.

Think of it this way: your intuition is a muscle, it's just an energetic one rather than a physical one. So if you had been exercising your body regularly, and were fit and strong, and then you stop exercising for a long time, what happens? You still have your muscles, sure. But if you go to try to exercise again, you will have a hard time. Your muscles need to be trained again in order for you to recover your fitness as it used to be.

It's the same with Reiki. If you had been exercising your intuition by practicing Reiki regularly, and then you stop, it will take some regular, mindful practice for you to feel the energy with the same intensity as you once did. But it's there - your intuition never goes away - it is a part of you. You just need to reestablish the connection and strengthen it again.

You might wonder if you need to be attuned again. There is no harm in doing this, as it may "jump start" your connection again. But you can achieve the same results by practicing Reiki for a few minutes every day.

What other books do you recommend to learn more about Reiki?

Reiki False Beliefs Exposed for All: Misinformation Kept Secret by a Few Revealed by Steve Murray

This book helps set straight many accepted but false ideas about Reiki.

Earthing: The Most Important Health Discovery Ever? By Clinton Ober, Stephen T. Sinatra, M.D., and Martin Zucker

This book gives a scientific view, supported by studies, of the health benefits of grounding. The Earth energy described in this book is that which combines with the Reiki energy when using Practical Reiki.

You Are Energy by Connie Dohan

This book presents a clear, concise guide to chakras, meridians, auras and the energetic aspects of disease. It's brief, friendly, informative, and to the point.

Ultimate Balance: Infusing the Vibrational Energy of Essential Oils into Chakras, Meridians and Organs by LeAnne Deardeuff, DC

This is more than a guide to essential oils, it is a detailed reference book showing major and minor organs, muscles, acupressure points, chakras, and clear explanations of the emotions associated with each, and symptoms and treatments for when the organs are off balance energetically.

Hands of Light: A Guide to Healing Through the Human Energy Field by Barbara Ann Brennan

This is the college course on all things energy. Read it to deepen your knowledge. It's deep and detailed, profound and wise. Everyone involved with energy healing should own a copy.

APPENDIX A
QUICK REFERENCE GUIDE TO PRACTICAL
REIKI ™

Here are some useful reference sheets for teaching or learning Practical Reiki.

Practical Reiki Level 1 Healings

- Self healing

- Situation/Qualities healing

- Healing for others

  o Local hands on healing

  o Distance healing

    ▪ Real time

    ▪ Preset

    ▪ Queued

- Cleansing a room

- Karmic Band healing

Practical Reiki Level 2 Healing

- Practical Reiki Cleansing

    o   Daily for at least a week

Practical Reiki Level 3 (Master) Healings

- Causal Healing

- Crystalline Healing (two sessions)

- DNA Healing

- Location Healing

- Birth Trauma Healing

- Past Life Healing (three sessions)

- Balance

*Before doing any level 3 healings on another or giving attunements, the series must be completed on oneself.

The Reiki Precepts

The secret method of inviting blessings
The spiritual medicine of many illnesses
For today only, do not anger, do not worry.
Be grateful. Honestly do your work. Be kind to all people.
In the morning and at night, with hands held in prayer,
think this in your mind, chant this with your mouth.
The Usui Reiki method to change your mind and body
for the better.

The founder, Mikao Usui

The briefest form:

Just for today:
Avoid anger
Avoid worry
Work honestly
Be grateful
Be kind.

Instruction to give to those receiving distance healing:

- Sit, recline, or lie down comfortably in a quiet place, with hands resting palms-up.

- Intend once in thoughts to receive the Reiki healing sent by (practitioner's name).

- Simply place a gentle awareness on how you feel, and observe all sensations with a sense of wonder. No effort is needed. Just "be in the moment."

Instruction for students receiving attunements:

- Sit, recline, or lie down comfortably in a quiet place, with hands resting palms-up.

- Intend once in thoughts to receive the Practical Reiki level (number) attunement.

- Simply place a gentle awareness on how you feel, and observe all sensations with a sense of wonder. No effort is needed. Just "be in the moment." You may wish to keep your eyes closed until the attunement comes to an end.

Procedure for Giving Attunements:

- Ask for protection and assistance from Spirit, guides, angels, etc.

- Connect with Reiki energy

- Intend, "Life force energy will be generated and will not fade until this attunement is complete."

- Intend "Practical Reiki level (number) attunement for (name)" (If by distance, queue the attunement if desired).

- Ask for assistance from recipient's guides, angels, etc. and add your own intention for recipient to be completely attuned.

- Place hands on recipient's shoulders for 20-30 seconds (if in person).

- Quietly be in the energy until it stops flowing.

- Ask the recipient for feedback when the attunement is finished for him/her.

APPENDIX B

ADDITIONAL INFORMATION FOR REFERENCE

Using a Pendulum to Check Chakras

A pendulum is a string or chain with a weighted object on one end. The object could be a charm from a necklace, a screw, a crystal, or almost any object, usually with a pointed end. The pendulum is used to get answers from one's highest self; answers that may not be obvious to the conscious mind.

To use a pendulum to check whether chakras are blocked, open, or overactive, follow these easy steps:

1) With the subject lying down, hold the pendulum from the end of the chain, between your middle finger and thumb. Dangle the weighted part over the area at the top of the subject's head, where the crown chakra is located.

2) Observe the pendulum. Chakras on the front of the body have energy that spins counter-clockwise. If the pendulum starts to move in counter-clockwise circles, observe the speed and size of the circles.

3) Move down to the third eye chakra in the center of the forehead and dangle the pendulum over that area.

4) Observe the pendulum, as before. Note the spin, speed and movement. Compare it with the way it moved over the crown chakra.

5) Repeat moving down to each chakra in turn (throat, heart, solar plexus, sacral, and base). Note which chakras caused the fastest, widest, or smallest amount of pendulum movement.

6) Offer the subject Reiki. Then test again to compare the difference afterward.

Ascended Master Kuthumi

Ole Gabrielsen, the founder of Kundalini Reiki, on which Practical Reiki is based, channeled this healing method during his meditations. While doing so, Gabrielsen received assistance from a Higher being, Ascended Master Kuthumi. During meditation, Kuthumi gave Gabrielsen methods for working with this energy and guidance how to teach it to others.

Because Practical Reiki is based on Kundalini Reiki, Master Kuthumi may be called upon to assist with Reiki healings or attunements to the Practical Reiki method as well.

Here is some information on Master Kuthumi, shared with permission from Kuthumi.com:

"In his last known incarnation, the Master Kuthumi lived and taught during the late 19th Century. He reportedly worked with Madame Blavatsky and the founders of Theosophy.

Kuthumi can be called on to help individuals to clear, to become conscious about their experience, to become more aware of what they want and what they are trying to accomplish in their evolutionary process."

More information on Master Kuthumi is available at Kuthumi.com and MasterKuthumi.com, among others.

ABOUT THE AUTHOR

Alice Langholt is a parent and teacher with Master level training in several Reiki modalities. She is an Associate at Insight Learning and Wellness Center, where she teaches locally in the Cleveland, Ohio area. Alice created an Energy Healing Certification Program, which is taught locally and online, offering intensive instruction in advanced techniques in energy healing over nine months. Alice has created Ebooks in Distance Healing and Energetic Protection, as well as specific coursework in Reiki for Parents, Reiki for Nurses and Caregivers (approved by the Ohio Board of Nurses for continuing education units), and more. She offers Reiki to patients and staff at The Cleveland Clinic, and is a Group Leader with The Distance Healing Network (the-dhn.com). Alice is rated the #1 most influential person on Twitter under the category Reiki by wefollow.com. Her husband, Evan, and their four kids know & use Reiki.

As a teacher, Alice believes that close guidance and mentoring are essential elements for learning energy healing. She provides this support to each student, getting to know each and assist him or her in growing intuition and becoming confident practitioners.

Find Alice at ReikiAwakening.com, and interact with her via @ReikiAwakening on Twitter, and Reiki Awakening on Facebook.

71353223R00076

Made in the USA
Columbia, SC
26 May 2017